# The Fruit Book

*Also by Mary Norwak*

BEGINNER'S GUIDE TO HOME FREEZING
THE COMPLETE BOOK OF BARBECUES
THE PIE BOOK

# The Fruit Book

MARY NORWAK

*Illustrations by Chris Evans*

London
MICHAEL JOSEPH

First published in Great Britain by Michael Joseph Ltd
52 Bedford Square, London, W.C.1.
1976



ISBN 0 7181 1514 7

Set and printed in Great Britain by
Northumberland Press Ltd, Gateshead
and bound by
Dorstel Press Ltd, Essex.

# Contents

# Introduction

Fruit is one of our most delicious and refreshing foods, always available to give a sparkle to meals. While most fruits are at their best freshly picked and eaten raw, they can also be used as the basis of hundreds of sweet and savoury dishes. Garden gluts and bargains at the greengrocers encourage the homely arts of jamming, bottling, freezing and pickle-making to supplement the often heavy and indigestible foods of winter.

It makes good sense to grow at least some of our own fruit these days. Even a tiny garden can sustain a few soft fruit bushes, perhaps an apple or pear tree, a row of raspberries, a blackberry cane, and a strawberry bed. Apart from the cheapness and freshness of home-grown fruit, there is the pleasure of having many varieties which are rapidly disappearing from our shops. Few greengrocers stock more than the most basic apples and pears and imported fruits. These days it is virtually impossible to buy eating gooseberries, cooking Morello cherries, redcurrants and greengages, and the old-fashioned medlars, quinces and mulberries only come from well-established gardens. Shop fruit is rarely cheap enough to use for making jam or preserving, so a little investment in plants and gardening time can pay rich rewards.

Before experimenting with the recipes in this book, take a little time to read the dictionary of fruit which I have given as a guide to the basic ways of dealing with each fruit, with particular attention to the flavours which complement each other. There is nothing more dreary than a bowl of plums stewed in water and served with packet custard. There are few things more delectable than plums cooked in the oven with layers of sugar and a mere sprinkling of water, chilled and flavoured with cherry brandy, sprinkled with almonds and topped with thick cream.

**Each recipe will give 4-6 servings, according to appetite.**

(1)

# A Dictionary of Fruit

This dictionary covers all the fruit likely to be found in gardens or in greengrocers in reasonable quantities. A few exotic imported fruits may be found in urban areas but these are not of general interest and must be excluded for reasons of space.

APPLES

Forget about the unappetising green monsters which masquerade as 'cooking apples'. The best apples to choose for cooking are hard and sweet, so use 'eaters' when they are in the prime.

For simple apple dishes, cook with butter instead of water when the pudding is to be eaten hot. Cut apples in thin slices, and cook gently in butter and sugar in a frying pan (allow 2 oz. butter and 4 tablespoons caster sugar to 2 lb. apples). Cook until the apples are golden and transparent, turning them gently and trying not to break the slices, then serve with cream. These apples make a delicious filling for a flan case made from sweet short pastry.

When apples tend to break up in cooking, mash them into a purée and use this sauce for a variety of sweet dishes. Try serving well-chilled apple purée with chopped nuts, a sprinkling of sugar, thick cream and shortbread biscuits. Or try it with old-fashioned sticky gingerbread and a blob of cream. Use apple purée in a sponge flan, top with soft fruit or canned fruit, and glaze with a little melted apple jelly or apricot jam.

Apples respond to a wide variety of complementary flavourings. They can be enhanced by cinnamon, cloves or nutmeg; pair well with blackberries, quinces and apricots, and can be flavoured with rum, lemon verbena or rose geranium leaves, lemon or orange rind and juice, and rosehip jelly. A little grated apple gives a great lift to horseradish sauce to serve with beef, while apples are also good cooked with pheasant, goose and pork, or served as a sauce. To end a meal, of course, there is nothing so delicious as a crisp dessert apple with a glass of port or sherry, while an apple or piece of apple pie make the traditional accompaniment to farmhouse Cheddar cheese.

### APRICOT

A freshly picked ripe apricot is one of the most delectable summer fruit, but fruit from the shops is rarely large and ripe enough to eat raw. Apricots are best poached in a heavy sugar syrup, or simmered in the oven with a sprinkling of sugar in a lidded casserole. Apricots go particularly well with Kirsch, Curaçao, rum, Crème de Noyau and almonds, and can be mixed with apples in pies and puddings. Apricots alone make delicious compote, ice cream, jam and soufflés, while grilled fresh or canned apricots are an accompaniment to ham and pork.

### AVOCADO

The avocado or alligator pear is a sub-tropical fruit, dark green and pear-shaped, with a slightly rough skin and large conical seed. It is rich in vitamins and oil, while the sugar and carbohydrate contents are very low; this richness has caused the avocado to be nicknamed 'midshipman's butter' by sailors in tropical waters, and 'poor man's butter' in Central America.

The fruit can be used for a variety of spreads, dressings and savoury dishes, and is particularly good for the appetiser course. One avocado will serve two people. To test for ripeness, the thumb and forefinger should be applied as to a peach. If the fruit 'gives' or feels soft, the avocado is ready for serving. Tomatoes bring out the flavour, and also fresh lime or lemon juice. Lemon juice also prevents discolouration if the fruit is prepared some time before a meal.

The avocado may be most simply served by being cut in half lengthwise, and the stone removed. Each half is then sprinkled with salt and pepper, or sugar and vinegar, lemon or orange juice. A half avocado can also be served with 1 tablespoon of sherry poured into the cavity left by the stone.

The pulp of the fruit can be scooped from the skin, seasoned with salt and pepper, and served on hot buttered toast. Seasoned with lemon juice, the pulp can be spread on small salt cocktail biscuits.

BANANA

The banana is a popular dessert fruit with a high calorific content, and it is particularly enjoyed by children. Some people like bananas mashed with sugar and cream, or jam, honey or chocolate. In America, the banana is often used with meat or poultry—particularly chicken—or is made into pies, fritters or ices. Cooked bananas lose much of their flavour, but are popular in West Indian cooking, and their natural accompaniments seem to be brown sugar and rum. Other complementary flavourings include brandy, ginger, walnuts, lemon rind and juice.

BLACKBERRY

A blackberrying expedition is always a good excuse for an autumn family outing, and the results can be turned to popular account in delicious puddings and unusual preserves. The largest sweet cultivated blackberries are of course very good served fresh with sugar and cream, and these are usually the best kind to use for open tarts. The wild blackberry, which has such a good flavour for preserves, usually needs sieving as the pips may irritate the very old and the very young. The flavour of both types of fruit is greatly enhanced by the use of a little rosewater (easily obtained from the chemists) or a couple of rose geranium leaves. Blackberries are natural companions for apples and quinces.

BLACKCURRANT

The blackcurrant gives one of the most popular of today's fruit flavours. The fruit is excellent for jams and syrups, and for all kinds of puddings, pies, ices and fools. A dash of Cassis, the blackcurrant liqueur, strengthens the flavour of ices and fools in particular, while a pinch of cinnamon complements the flavour if put into the pastry of pies and flans.

BLUEBERRY

The wild blueberry, bilberry or whortleberry grows on moors and heathlands and used to be sold in commercial quantities. This dark blue berry with a soft greyish bloom is widely cultivated in America and Eastern Europe, and today's supplies are mostly imported fresh or frozen, or bottled in syrup.

The sharp flavour is distinctive, and the blueberry is particularly good in pies and made into jam.

### CHERRY

While there are many different types of cherries, they are usually known in the shops as black or white eating cherries. For cooking purposes, the Morello sour cherry is most often used, but it is difficult to buy and must usually be home-grown. The flavour of cherries is popular for tarts and compotes and black cherries make a very special jam. Cherry brandy and cherry gin are other favourites. Their flavour in recipes is enhanced by brandy, Kirsch and cherry brandy. While cherries are normally eaten as dessert fruit, a cherry sauce is often served with duck, and can also be used for turbot.

### CRANBERRY

Cranberries have almost become an American prerogative, but in fact they grow well in many places in the British Isles and are particularly used in Scotland. In Scandinavia too, a favourite dish is pancakes with cranberry jam. The slightly tart quality of the fruit makes appetite-stimulating sauces and relishes which are normally served with turkey, but are also good with most meats, particularly pork and ham. Cinnamon and cloves help to bring out the flavour, and oranges are often combined with cranberries. In addition to their use in savoury dishes, cranberries are also delicious made into rather unusual puddings, which particularly appeal in winter when sharply-refreshing fruit is not always easily available.

### DAMSON AND SLOE

The small round dark blue damson (and its wild cousin, the sloe) have a delicious and distinctive flavour which used to be very popular in the kitchen, although not often eaten raw. Damsons are particularly suitable for tarts, puddings and pies, for jams and jellies and for fruit fools and whips. Both damsons and sloes were also used extensively for making such drinks as damson brandy and sloe gin, and for spiced fruits to eat with savoury dishes.

### FIG

Figs are at their best freshly picked as they are highly perishable. They should be soft to the touch with a light fragrant scent. They are delicious straight from the tree, or can be peeled, sliced and served with cream. A little lemon or orange juice may be used with them, or a few drops of Kirsch or rum. Fresh figs are not usually cooked, although they can be bottled in syrup or frozen, and recipes usually use dried figs. Fresh figs can however be made into jam or chutney.

### GOOSEBERRY

Gooseberries are little eaten anywhere else in the world but England, but they have been popular here for centuries, perhaps because they can be easily grown and can be used while still green and hard. They formed one of the traditional Whitsun dishes. A large ripe eating gooseberry is delicious, but most varieties are picked young and green for tarts, puddings and pies, jamming, bottling and freezing. The gooseberry is popular for making fools and hot puddings, but is also often used to make sauce for savoury dishes. When using gooseberries for sweet dishes, a head of elder flowers cooked with the fruit gives a delightful muscat flavour.

### GRAPE

There are dozens of varieties of grapes, but for cooking purposes they are usually simply divided into black, white and seedless sultana grapes. While they are normally eaten fresh and ripe as dessert fruit, peeled white muscat grapes are used for garnishing sole, and also for an excellent stuffing and garnish for pheasant.

### GRAPEFRUIT

The grapefruit is a refreshing variety of citrus fruit with a slight tang which makes it particularly useful for appetising first courses and fruit salads. It can be used in many ways like the orange, but does not benefit from cooking, although a little grapefruit in a marmalade recipe gives a good flavour. When grapefruit is used in a salad or as an ice, a little chopped mint is a pleasant garnish.

GREENGAGE

The greengage is the sweetest and best of all eating plums, sticky with juice. They are delicious preserved in syrup, and are complemented by the flavour of Benedictine. If there are enough to be cooked, greengages make delicious jam and are good in tarts and puddings.

LEMON

Lemons provide one of the most popular of all kitchen flavourings. Lemon rind and juice are indispensable in a huge variety of recipes from salad dressings and savouries through to cakes and ices. A squeeze of lemon juice enhances fish and veal, is essential to mayonnaise and gives a zip to pastry. Lemon juice helps in the preparation of such fruit as melons, apples, plums and rhubarb, and helps to preserve the delicate colouring of peaches and avocadoes. It is also a useful addition to such puddings as treacle tart where it counteracts the sweetness.

LIME

A distinctively-flavoured fruit similar to a lemon but greenish in colouring. Bottled lime juice is easily obtainable, but the fresh fruit is not often imported. A slice of lime makes a pleasant change from lemon in drinks, and limes used in marmalade are delicious.

LOGANBERRY

The loganberry is similar to a raspberry, but has a slightly acid flavour like the mulberry. Loganberries are really better cooked than raw, and can be used for any raspberry, blackberry or mulberry recipe. They are particularly good used in apple dishes, such as a loganberry and apple charlotte, and mix well with other summer fruit such as strawberries, gooseberries and raspberries to give a rich colour and sharp flavour to Summer Pudding, and to jams.

MEDLAR

Medlars are like large round rose-hips, ne colour of unripe brown russet apples and very hard. They should be left on the tree until November if there are no hard frosts, picked when quite dry and stored indoors. They are then stored for some weeks until semi-rotten or 'bletted' before eating. They used to be eaten with a glass of port, or can be used to make wine, fruit cheese, or jelly to serve with game. The soft brown flesh can be mashed with thick cream and brown sugar to eat. Medlars can also be baked in a shallow ovenware dish with butter and cloves, and served like baked apples with sugar and cream.

### MELON

Many varieties of melon are available, according to the season of the year, although most are imported during the summer. The cantaloupe melon has a ribbed, warty skin and flesh which is either dark orange or pale green, juicy and sweet. The smaller honeydew melon has a lace-patterned pale skin and is more watery and sweet. The Charantais melon looks like a miniature pumpkin, has a rich orange flesh and a strong musky scent and flavour. The water melon comes from very hot countries and is like a large dark-green football with bright pink flesh and dark brown seeds scattered throughout. It is very watery and refreshing, with little flavour.

While melons are occasionally cooked as a vegetable, or made into jam or pickles, they are best served well chilled at the beginning or end of a meal. The flesh blends well with oranges and the two fruits can be combined in a refreshing cocktail. Melon can be eaten alone with a little sugar and nutmeg or ginger, but is more refreshing served with a little salt and even pepper. Lemon rind and juice can also be used with melon, or a few drops of Crème de Cacao or port. A slice of melon is excellent with cold pork or ham, particularly raw Parma ham, and it is also good with Roquefort cheese.

### MULBERRY

The mulberry was formerly grown for the sake of its leaves upon which silkworms feed. The best tree for this purpose however is the white mulberry which yields nearly white berries which are small, sweet and flavourless. The best eating mulberry is the black mulberry, which has delicious fruit to eat raw or to cook. The fruit is similar to a loganberry, and slightly tart, and is at its best eaten with sugar and cream; the juice stains hands and clothes very badly. The mulberry can be used in recipes for raspberries and loganberries. It is particularly good made into a pie to serve with cream or junket, and makes excellent jam.

### NECTARINE

This smooth-skinned variety of peach is rarely seen, but is a delicious dessert fruit. It is smaller than a peach, with firmer flesh and richer flavour. The nectarine can be used in all recipes for peaches, but is really too good and rare to cook.

### ORANGE

The orange is one of the most popular of everyday fruit with its fresh flavour and multitude of uses, and though formerly confined to the winter season, it is now obtainable all the year round. Sweet oranges in recipes can be enhanced by the orange-flavoured liqueurs, Curaçao, Cointreau and Grand Marnier, and by rum and gin. Oranges blend particularly well with cranberries, quinces, rhubarb and apples, while a flavouring of orange rind or juice does wonders for duck, veal and for beef stews. An orange salad, or baked oranges also make a good accompaniment for ham or pork, and a garnish of freshly chopped mint is the perfect finish.

### PEACH

There can be few things more delicious than a huge ripe sticky peach eaten in the hot sunshine. Too often though, shop peaches are small and somewhat hard and only fit for cooking or preserving. Luckily, fresh peach jam, spiced peaches and peaches in brandy are all very worth making and tasting. Canned peaches are with us all the time, but peach slices are rarely worth eating. Sometimes a good brand of whole or half peaches can be found, and canned white peaches are worth looking for since they retain the texture and slight sharpness of the fresh fruit. Fresh or canned peaches respond well to the help of brandy, rum, white wine, Maraschino and peach brandy, and they are one of the fruits which pair well with savoury food. Try them with cream cheese, and with pork, ham and bacon dishes.

PEAR

True dessert pears are juicy and sweet, but many varieties are only suitable for cooking, not because they are acid but lacking in flavour. These are best cooked in red wine or a sugar syrup. They are best of all if halved, peeled and cored, pierced with cloves and cooked in a casserole with wine or syrup. Small hard winter cooking pears can be cooked for hours in red wine in the slowest oven until they are mahogany-coloured and tender, and delicious served with thick cream. Apart from cloves, pears blend well with cinnamon, or can be cooked with a few pieces of quince for a delicate flavour. Chocolate sauce makes a good accompaniment, or toasted walnuts, and a dash of rum in any pear dish makes it really special. A fresh juicy pear is delicious eaten with a piece of Camembert or Brie.

PINEAPPLE

The pineapple, traditional symbol of hospitality, is also one of the most delicious of dessert fruits. A simple slice of pineapple can be served sprinkled with Kirsch, or a half pineapple makes a container for ice cream, or even for a sweet-and-savoury salad. Fresh pineapple has the finest flavour, but the canned fruit is useful for recipes although rather insipid in flavour. For a dish which requires gelatine, canned pineapple should always be used, as fresh pineapple contains an enzyme which inhibits the setting quality of gelatine. For sweet dishes, pineapple is enhanced by rum as well as Kirsch, and for ending a meal a piece of fresh pineapple is delicious with Roquefort cheese. Those who like a combination of savoury flavours with fruit find that pineapple enhances the flavour of ham, pork, chicken and shrimps.

PLUM

There are many varieties of plum, and many such as the popular Victoria are delicious to eat raw. The little Mirabelle or cherry plum is another favourite, very popular in Europe for preserves and drinks. Plainly stewed plums can be very boring however, but are improved with a dash of cinnamon, a little lemon or orange rind and juice, or a sprinkling of flaked almonds. A dash of cherry brandy or a little red wine in the cooking will also add richness. The most delicious way of cooking plums is to layer them in a fireproof casserole with caster sugar and a piece of cinnamon stick, half-cover with water, and leave in a slow oven (300°F or Gas Mark 2) until they are tender and the juice is running.

### QUINCE

The quince is an oddly-shaped round or pear-shaped fruit with yellow woolly skin and yellow flesh which turns pink during cooking. The fruit is slightly sharp and very strongly scented and flavoured, and has mucilaginous seeds which help to give a firm set to jams and jellies. Quinces may be cooked on their own, or added to dishes containing apples (usually one quince is enough to give a distinctive flavour to an apple pie or a batch of apple jelly). Try using them with pears and blackberries too, or flavour quince dishes with lemon or orange rind and juice, cloves or port. The Japanese quince or Japonica commonly grown as an ornamental shrub has fruits like quinces, which are very hard to peel but can be used to make quince jelly.

### RASPBERRY

The raspberry must be the most perfect of all fruit, delectable when fresh yet retaining colour and flavour when preserved. They are beautiful served plainly with sugar and cream, or with a sprinkling of claret, Sauternes or Champagne. They blend well with other fruit, particularly peaches, rhubarb, strawberries and redcurrants, and are enhanced by a dash of Kirsch. A pinch of cinnamon in raspberry dishes is unusual but good, while a pinch of freshly-ground coffee in the pastry of raspberry tarts is superb. Raspberries, like most other fruit, are horrid when 'stewed' and so are not at their best when bottled, though they may be improved by bottling in a mixture with blackcurrants and eating gooseberries to make a winter fruit salad. They make delicious jam however, freeze beautifully, and are particularly good for making syrups and cordials.

### REDCURRANT AND WHITE CURRANT

These fruits are too seldom seen, although easily grown. Fresh red- and white currants are delicious served with nothing but a sprinkling of sugar. They are also excellent mixed with raspberries (a bowl of frozen redcurrants and raspberries can be very refreshing in the middle of winter), or in a four-fruit mixture with raspberries, strawberries and eating gooseberries, or with a few blackcurrants added. When the fruit is cooked, it tends to be 'pippy', but redcurrants give a distinctive flavour to ice cream, and make excellent jelly to serve with mutton, veal, hare or venison. This jelly also makes a useful glaze for a variety of cakes and flans. Redcurrant juice gives flavour and setting quality to strawberry jam.

White currants may be used as redcurrants, and make a beautiful preserve set in their own jelly.

### RHUBARB

Rhubarb is much maligned, but the first early young pink sticks are delicious after stodgy winter food. The thicker sticks of summer are best used for preserves, and are excellent for chutney and jam. Rhubarb is not suitable for eating uncooked, and is best prepared without any water—there is nothing more dismal than pieces of stringy rhubarb floating in a weak solution of sugar and water. For the very best flavour, cut the rhubarb into chunks and cook in the oven or on the stove in nothing more than some raspberry or plum jam, or some marmalade until just tender. The colour and flavour are then delectable. Lemon, orange, angelica and raspberry are complementary flavours, and rhubarb makes good jams used as the bulk ingredient with oranges or dried fruits such as figs and dates.

### STRAWBERRY

Most people enjoy strawberries plainly served with caster sugar and cream. The tiny alpine strawberry has the best and most delicate flavour, and is better without cream. All varieties are best eaten freshly gathered, and some people then eat them with just a pinch of salt, or even a shake of pepper. Strawberries are also delicious served in orange juice, or with claret or Champagne poured over them. They also respond well to many liqueurs such as Benedictine, Cointreau, Crème de Noyau, Curaçao, Grand Marnier and Maraschino. Port is another favourite for pouring over or serving with them. Strawberries and raspberries blend together surprisingly well in dishes, and are worth mixing when supplies of both are short. The strawberry changes drastically in flavour and texture when processed by cooking or preserving in any way, although a frozen strawberry purée retains the fresh fruit flavour. Strawberry jam however is one of the most popular preserves.

TANGERINE

This is one of the few really seasonal fruit in these days of advanced preservation, reminding us that citrus fruit used to be a prized Christmas treat. This small orange has a loose rind and very sweet juice, and a distinctive flavour. Today it is largely superseded by two similar fruit, the clementine and the satsuma. All three make delicious marmalade and can be blended with vanilla ice cream to give a delicious ice which is excellent served with Christmas pudding.

(2)

# What to Grow and How to Grow It

These gardening notes are intended as a simple guide to the kind of fruit which can be grown in most gardens, with the most basic cultural instructions and guidance on the best varieties to choose. When you have made your choice, go to a well-established nursery, even if you pay more for plants. A good nursery will provide the best plant for your purpose, properly pruned and in good condition. If you go to a fairly local nursery, you should be able to get information on the type of soil and situation for your plants since they will be close to the conditions in which the nursery has prepared them for sale. Cheap plants are seldom worth buying and may yield inferior fruit or a badly shaped tree, or be of a type unsuitable for your garden. Check with a book on fruit-growing to see how plants should be pruned or trained from year to year, and if feeding is necessary.

APPLE

There are dozens of varieties of apples to choose from, but it is probably wisest with a small garden to choose one or two eating apples which yield crisp slices and are also excellent for cooking, and one cooking apple which yields fluffy purée. The apples like a dry situation with plenty of sunshine and should be sheltered from strong winds and from late spring frosts. They may be grown as bushes or as cordon trees, although older larger gardens often have enormous standard trees. The soil should not be too rich and fertile or the tree becomes lush and yields delayed and poor crops. Apples grow well in grass which conserves moisture in summer and uses surplus nitrogen which is not needed for apples. Three-year-old trees should be planted but will not start bearing until well-established about eighteen months later.

Try planting George Cave for an early dessert apple which is excellent for small gardens. James Grieve is a September dessert apple which is also good for cooking. Monarch is an October cooker but matures well into an eating apple from December onwards. Golden Noble is an October yellow-fleshed cooking apple which is frothy and needs little sweetening. Sunset is a good October dessert apple which tastes like a Cox but is easier to grow.

### APRICOT

The apricot is a hardy tree but flowers early, often in February, and so is subject to frost. The best position for a tree is on a warm, sheltered south or west wall, allowing a space about 15 feet wide by 9 feet high.

Only one tree is needed, as the apricot is self-fertile. Soil need not be rich, but some bonemeal should be forked into the soil before planting. Order a two- or three-year-old fan-trained tree, but do not expect the tree to bear until its fourth year, and certainly not in the first year after planting. The apricot has shallow feeding roots which are easily damaged, and it is a good idea to conserve soil moisture in the summer with a mulch of compost around the tree. Flowers should be protected on possibly frosty nights by hanging some soft fabric in front of the tree. On sunny days, pollen can be transferred between flowers with a small paintbrush.

Moorpark is a favourite variety which is vigorous and free fruiting, producing large fruit at the end of August.

### BLACKBERRY

A blackberry cane takes up a lot of space but yields a large crop. Plant in a medium to heavy soil which keeps moist in summer and is slightly acid. Varieties which fruit in September should be in a sunny place so that all the fruit ripens, but earlier varieties can be grown in partial shade. If possible, plant against a fence about 5 feet high, or against horizontal wires stretched between posts. The blackberry fruits on the previous year's growth which should be cut at ground level as soon as the crop is finished. Keep the current year's growth separate from the fruiting stems or they will become entangled and possibly damaged and it may become difficult to pick the fruit.

Himalaya Giant is a strong plant with enormous crops but it needs a lot of room. Merton Thornless is easier to control, but needs richer soil, and the berries are plump, sweet and juicy. Bedford Giant is an earlier cropper which yields well but the flavour is not so good.

BLACKCURRANT

Blackcurrants like fairly heavy soil with plenty of organic manure; if the soil is poor and dry, the fruit will also be poor and dry. The fruit grows on new wood each year, and the old wood should be cut out after fruiting. Plant two-year-old bushes about 4 feet apart in a place which is sheltered from north and east winds, where insects will pollinate the flowers. When the plant is put in, cut the stems back to 6 inches so that the bush gets established in the first year and starts bearing the following season. The young feeding roots are near the surface and should not be allowed to dry out, nor should they be disturbed by digging.

Plant Boskoop Giant for early large fruit and very long bunches, but see it is in a sheltered place. Wellington is a mid-season cropper with a consistent heavy yield of high quality fruit.

CHERRY

The cherry tree is very large, and trees need to be planted together as they need different varieties for pollination. The exception to this is the acid Morello cherry which is excellent for cooking and preserving, is self-fertile, and a good pollinator for sweet varieties. Cherries will grow in most parts of the country, but are not suitable for areas which experience late frosts. They like soil with plenty of lime, which is well drained. Buy four-year-old trees as the framework of the tree will be established by then, and cherries do not bear fruit until six years old. Sweet cherries may be gathered as early as June, but the Morello lasts through until September.

Merton Favourite is a large black early cherry with sweet rich fruit and it can be pollinated by Merton Bigarreau or Morello. Merton Bigarreau is a mid-July dark-red cherry. The Morello is a red acid cooking variety which is most useful in the kitchen.

FIG

Fig trees succeed best in warm areas, but do not always ripen well. A fan-trained tree against a wall is best, or it can be planted against a wall at the back of a cold lean-to greenhouse. Figs need poor soil and a restricted root run, so they are best grown in a large tub, or in a pit lined with concrete, iron sheets or bricks, and they should not be fed. If a tree is fed and given a lot of soil, its branches are sappy and easily destroyed by frost. The fruit is formed during the summer, so must be protected during the winter by sacking or straw.

The best varieties to grow are either Brown Turkey or Brunswick, with large well-flavoured, reddish-brown fruit.

### GOOSEBERRY

The gooseberry grows well almost anywhere, but likes potash in the soil. The bushes will grow in half-shade which can be useful in a small garden. Dig the soil deeply before planting to give good drainage and dig in some complete fertiliser. It is best to order three-year-old bushes which can be planted through the winter if the soil is not frozen or waterlogged. Most people grow gooseberries as bushes, and base suckers should be removed and the centre of the bush kept open for easier picking. The fruit can be picked while still green but of usable size, or fruit can be left until larger.

Whinhams Industry is a good variety for all-round crops as it can be used small and young for cooking, then left to ripen for eating as dessert fruit. Careless is a vigorous heavy-cropping variety for cooking, while Leveller is a large yellow dessert berry.

### GRAPE

Grapes can be grown outdoors in warm areas, or in a cold greenhouse or conservatory. The outdoor vine needs a sunny position not only to ripen the fruit but to ripen the growth of the plant and toughen it against winter frost. A fairly poor soil is best as rich soil will encourage soft growth. If possible, grow a vine on a south or west wall on well-drained soil, with clay subsoil broken up, and a little gravel or mortar rubble dug in. Two-year-old pot-grown plants can be ordered for outdoors and the plant should be surrounded by peat and kept well-watered for a year or two until it is well-established. Grapes need careful training, and the fruit bunches need restricting and the berries reducing, but a little care ensures large ripe fruit.

Black Hamburg is the best choice for a cold greenhouse and for a sheltered wall. Siegerrebe is an outdoor variety with large golden fruit ripening in October.

LOGANBERRY

Plant a loganberry cane in a sunny position in open ground or against a south or west fence. Use plenty of organic matter in the soil to retain moisture in the summer. Loganberries like a slightly acid soil, and a fairly thick layer of peat spread around each plant in spring is helpful. Allow a space about 8 feet wide by 6 feet high for each plant, and plant firmly in the autumn. Cut the canes back to 6 inches from the ground to encourage strong new growth in the first year. If no fence is available, support the canes on four horizontal wires stretched between posts, and see the canes are arranged to receive the maximum light and air. The berries should not be picked when bright red but only when almost black as they will then have developed their full flavour.

Grow the certified virus-free variety LY59 and avoid thornless varieties which rarely crop well.

MEDLAR

Medlar trees like a rather moist soil, but need plenty of space as they are spreading trees. The Dutch medlar needs about 20 feet space across, but the Nottingham medlar is more upright and needs only half the space. The medlar is a very decorative tree with large white flowers and a weeping character, but the unusual fruit is not to everybody's taste.

MULBERRY

The Common or Black Mulberry (*Morus nigra*) is the one to grow for fruit, and the tree is very decorative. It grows fairly slowly but can reach 20 feet and has a rather heavy head. Old trees tend to fall almost to the ground yet they continue to grow. The mulberry likes a sunny, fairly sheltered garden, with soil which is neither waterlogged in winter nor baked hard in summer. If the tree is planted in short grass, it encourages earlier cropping and better crops than when planted in cultivated soil. The fruit begins to drop when it is ripe, and stains very badly. The best way to gather mulberries is to spread light polythene sheeting under the tree and shake the branches. Leave the sheeting in position while fruit remains on the tree as the ripe fruit will continue to fall.

### PEACH AND NECTARINE

The peach is slightly hardier than the nectarine, which has a smooth skin and fine flavour. Both trees may be grown under glass or against a wall, or even as bushes in open ground, but the trees flower early and are therefore likely to suffer frost damage. Ordinary garden soil is suitable if well-drained, but heavy clay needs plenty of compost worked in before planting. A little lime is also appreciated by the trees. Peaches and nectarines hate being moved so care should be taken over planting, which must take place immediately after delivery. Spread the roots out well and surround with peat about three inches deep to stop frost penetrating the roots. Fruit should be picked when fully ripe, and must be treated gently to avoid bruising.

Hale's Early is a good peach with large fruit which can be grown indoors or out. Peregrine fruits a week or two later in early August and is good for outdoor growing. Humboldt is a nectarine which is hardy with large fruit having a fine flavour.

### PEAR

While some old gardens have trees of the small hard winter cooking pears, it is more usual to plant dessert pears today. Pears bloom earlier than apples so are best protected from frost; they also appreciate being in a sun-trap when the fruit is ready to ripen. Pears grow well on walls, but a dwarf pyramid shape is neat and manageable for modern gardens. They prefer a richer soil than apples, and don't like heavy clay or shallow soil over chalk or sand. The trees are best planted in the autumn, and at least two varieties should be planted for cross-fertilisation. Pears should be harvested just before ripening, and they tend to ripen very quickly once stored—they need to be stored in a cool place which is frost-proof and inspected regularly.

Try growing the famous dessert pear Williams' Bon Chrétien, and Conference which is easy to grow and good for eating and cooking. A compact tree is Fondante d'Automne which is a reliable cropper with sweet juicy fruit, while Packham's Triumph is a small tree with fruit similar to Williams'.

### PLUM, GREENGAGE AND DAMSON

The different varieties of plums can be grown in most places, but are particularly successful in south-east England and the Midlands. Damsons are the hardiest type, and some greengages the most tender, but all are liable to be affected by spring frost damage since they flower in mid-April. Standard trees are large, and bush trees may be more suitable for small gardens, or fan-trained trees against a wall. They prefer a medium to heavy soil, if possible well-treated with organic manure. Many plums are self-fertile, but even these fruit better if another variety is planted nearby for good pollination. Plum branches break easily and may need supporting if the crop is heavy as harvest-time approaches.

Try Merryweather for a vigorous damson with large fruit, or Farleigh for a smaller variety yielding a large crop. Denniston's Superb is a greengage with a fine flavour which crops well in all districts and is a good wall tree. A variety of cooking and eating plums is worth planting. Try the delicious all-round Victoria which is a heavy cropper, Czar as a well-flavoured early cooker, Early Laxton for a cooking/dessert plum, and Marjorie's Seedling as a late cooking plum with an excellent flavour.

### QUINCE

Quinces grow best in the warmer south and west of Britain, and the ideal site is sheltered with moist soil but sunshine. A new tree should be planted no later than November and it is best to grow a bush rather than a standard tree since quinces spread and are difficult to shape well. Plant as for apples, and stake securely. During the first growing summer, water when necessary and in hot weather spray the foliage occasionally with clear water. Little pruning is needed except for the removal of crossed or weak branches.

Vranja and Portugal are the most common varieties. A newer type called Meech's Prolific has fruit with a smoother skin, and can start to fruit at only three years old.

### RASPBERRY

This is not a difficult fruit to grow and very rewarding since it is so good for preserving and freezing. Raspberries will grow in partial shade away from tree roots, but they like protection from winds. As they flower late, they are not likely to be spoiled by frost. A heavy or loamy soil is best with some organic fertiliser. The roots are shallow and spreading and need food and moisture during the fruiting season. Plant about 15 inches apart in rows, with the rows 4 feet apart, and cut down the canes to 6 inches when first planted. There will be no fruit the first year, but the canes will grow strongly for the following season. Don't dig near raspberries or their roots may be damaged; water them well in dry weather, and put down compost or peat along each side of the row. Raspberries need training along horizontal wires stretched between posts. The fruit can be gathered from early July, and some varieties carry on from September to November.

Malling Promise is a good all-round fruit for early summer, but the flavour is not the best. Malling Jewel is a mid-season fruit with superb flavour and vigorous canes. Norfolk Giant is a heavy cropping late summer fruit of high quality. Zeva is a new autumn variety which has to be cut down every spring, and fruit is borne on the growth made during the summer.

### REDCURRANT AND WHITE CURRANT

These are long-lived plants and well worth growing as the fruit is so rarely seen in the shops. A bush of both types grows more like a gooseberry than a blackcurrant, and they fruit on old wood. All types of soil are suitable provided they contain potash and phosphates, so bonfire ashes and bonemeal should be dug in before bushes are planted. The wood of the bushes is rather brittle and easily broken, so the plants should be sheltered from wind. Plant two-year-old bushes, about 4 feet apart with 5 feet between rows.

Grow Laxton's Red for a good crop of large high quality berries, or Red Lake, a heavy cropper. The best flavoured white variety is White Versailles.

RHUBARB

Light soil produces early crops, but the rhubarb will then need more feeding and watering. A fairly heavy garden soil should be deeply dug before planting, cleared of perennial weeds, and well manured before planting. The plants are bought as crowns with several buds or as sets consisting of single buds with short sections of root. Plant 2 feet apart, making sure the plants are deep enough for the topmost buds to be just covered. Don't pull stems from newly-planted rhubarb the first year, but build up the plants by watering well and feeding with liquid fertiliser. Early rhubarb can be forced by covering the stems with a large box, tea chest or bucket about mid-February so the first fruit can be pulled in March. The plants should be uncovered in April for later pickings.

Timperley Early is a very early variety with bright pink thin sticks. Victoria is a vigorous plant with good colour and flavour, and The Sutton is a strong variety for continuous summer cropping.

STRAWBERRY

Strawberries should be planted in a sunny position, although summer varieties will still ripen well if there is some shade during part of the day. Perpetual strawberries which fruit from August to October should have a position where they catch plenty of autumn sunshine. Alpine or wood strawberries are now popular and can be grown from seed, but the other two types of strawberries are better bought originally as plants. New plants can be grown from the 'runners' each year which spread out from the parent plant, and these can replace old plants as they become exhausted or infested with perennial weeds.

Cambridge Vigour is an early variety which can be grown under cloches. Cambridge Favourite is a mid-season fruit which crops over a long period and can be grown under cloches or in the open. Gento is a perpetual late-fruiting berry which is a heavy cropper with large fruit, but it needs good soil and generous watering. Baron Solemacher, Alexandria and Delicious are alpine strawberries with tiny richly-flavoured fruit which can be sown as seed in March, planted out in May and will begin to fruit in the autumn.

(3)

# First Courses

A fruit first course usually consists of a naked grapefruit half, a slice of melon with a sprinkling of ground ginger to make the unwary eater choke, or—horrifyingly—a bowl of canned grapefruit in heavy syrup. More daringly, an avocado pear may be offered with an oil-and-vinegar dressing, or a seafood filling, or a slice of raw ham may come with a piece of melon or a fresh fig. But fruit should be used with far more imagination to make a stimulating first course which tempts the palate without deadening the appetite.

It is worth trying cheese or cream cheese with fruit; using a seafood filling, or preparing a light salad, or even making a fruit soup. These unusual dishes are also useful on their own for a light luncheon or supper.

### APPLE SALAD

4 red eating apples
2 oz. chopped walnuts
1 stick celery
6 tablespoons mayonnaise
1 teaspoon lemon juice

Core the apples carefully and scoop out as much flesh as possible. Chop the apple flesh and mix with the nuts, chopped celery and mayonnaise. Return to the apple skins and sprinkle with lemon juice. Serve as a first course, or with thinly sliced ham or poultry.

### APPLE SOUP

1½ lb. cooking apples
¼ pint white wine
¼ pint single cream
sugar

Peel and core the apples and cut them into slices. Simmer in just enough water to cover until soft. Put through a sieve and add to the wine and cream. Sweeten very lightly, as the soup should be rather sharp to taste. Chill before serving.

### AVOCADO WITH SPICY TUNA SAUCE

7-oz. can tuna fish
5-oz. carton soured cream
4 teaspoons Worcestershire sauce
1 teaspoon tomato purée
1 small onion or 2 spring onions
salt
2 avocado pears
1 tablespoon lemon juice

Drain and roughly flake the tuna fish. Combine the soured cream, Worcestershire sauce, tomato purée, chopped onion and salt. Add tuna and stir together gently. Brush pear halves with lemon juice and place in serving dish. Pile filling into centre and garnish with some lemon wedges and parsley sprigs.

### CUBAN AVOCADO

1 clove of garlic
1 avocado
¼ teaspoon salt
¼ teaspoon chili powder
2 teaspoons finely minced onion
1 teaspoon lemon juice
mayonnaise

Rub a bowl with the cut garlic clove. Add salt, chili powder, onion and lemon juice to the mashed avocado pulp and place in the bowl. Cover with a thin layer of mayonnaise. Leave in a cold place, and stir well just before serving. Use as a canapé spread, a sauce for raw vegetables or a dressing for lettuce salads.

### AVOCADO CRAB SALAD

2 avocadoes
3 teaspoons lemon juice
4 oz. crabmeat (fresh or canned)
6 tablespoons mayonnaise
pinch of curry powder
2 tablespoons breadcrumbs
1 oz. butter

Cut the avocadoes in half, remove stones and brush surfaces with 2 teaspoons lemon juice. Bind crabmeat with mayonnaise, remaining teaspoon lemon juice and curry powder. Warm this mixture and fill avocado halves. Top with breadcrumbs and a dab of butter, and put under grill for 3 minutes.

### AVOCADO BACON ROLLS

4 large rashers bacon
2 avocadoes
whole cloves
4 slices buttered toast

Cut bacon into strips about 2 × 4 in. Scoop out large spoonfuls of avocado flesh and wrap each in a strip of bacon. Fix each bacon roll with a whole clove. Grill slowly till bacon is cooked, take out cloves, and serve on buttered toast.

### CHERRY SOUP

1½ lb. red eating cherries
1 orange
juice of 1 lemon
3 oz. sugar
½ pint red wine
1 dessertspoon arrowroot
5-oz. carton soured cream

Stone the cherries and put into a saucepan with the grated rind and juice of the orange, and the lemon juice and sugar. Add the wine and 1 pint water and simmer for 5 minutes. Remove from the heat. Mix the arrowroot with 1 tablespoon water and stir into the soup. Bring back to the boil and boil for 1 minute. Chill and serve with a spoonful of soured cream to garnish each bowl.

### CRANBERRY APPETISER

8 oz. cranberries
4 oz. sugar
2 tablespoons lemon or orange juice

Cook the cranberries in 1 pint water until the skins burst.

Sieve and add sugar, stirring until dissolved. Add the fruit juice and serve chilled.

### GRAPEFRUIT WITH SHRIMPS

2 grapefruit
8 oz. peeled shrimps
4 tablespoons mayonnaise
1 teaspoon chopped parsley

Cut the grapefruit in half. Remove sections of flesh without skin and then remove skin from the peel to leave a clean container. Mix the grapefruit flesh with the shrimps and mayonnaise, and return to the skins. Sprinkle with chopped parsley.

### GRAPEFRUIT STARTER

2 large grapefruit
½ oz. butter
2 oz. brown sugar
juice of 1 orange
1 oz. sultanas
2 oz. dates
½ teaspoon ground cinnamon

Cut the grapefruit into halves and remove the segments. Put butter, sugar, orange juice, sultanas, chopped dates and cinnamon into a saucepan and simmer for 5 minutes. Add the grapefruit and simmer for 2 minutes. Fill the grapefruit shells and serve at once.

### MELON AND LOBSTER COCKTAIL

1 small honeydew melon
8 oz. lobster (fresh, frozen or canned)
8 tablespoons mayonnaise
juice of ½ lemon

Peel the melon and cut the flesh into small pieces. Mix with the lobster and bind with the mayonnaise thinned with the lemon juice. Put into individual bowls and chill well before serving.

### ORANGE AND TOMATO SOUP

juice of 2 oranges
1 pint canned tomato juice
¼ pint white wine
1 teaspoon sugar
salt and pepper

Mix together all the ingredients and chill before serving. A little chopped fresh mint may be used as a garnish.

### PEACH APPETISERS

6 canned peach halves
2 oz. Roquefort cheese
1 oz. butter
¼ pint double cream
4 tablespoons cream cheese
lettuce leaves
paprika

If white peach halves are available, they are the most delicious for this dish. Mix the cheese and softened butter and stuff the hollows of the peach halves. Turn each peach half upside down on a lettuce leaf. Lightly whip the cream and fold in the cream cheese. Put on to the peaches and put a pinch of paprika on the top of each one. Serve very cold as a first course, or as a light luncheon dish.

### PRAWN-STUFFED PEARS

6 canned pear halves
lettuce leaves
4 oz. peeled prawns
8 oz. cottage cheese
1 teaspoon chopped chives
salt and pepper

Drain pears well and arrange on a bed of lettuce leaves. Cut each prawn into four pieces and blend into cottage cheese with chopped chives, salt and pepper to taste. Put a spoonful of mixture into each pear half and serve chilled as a first course, or a light summer luncheon.

### COTTAGE PEARS

16-oz. can pear halves
lettuce leaves
8 oz. cottage cheese
1 small onion
2 oz. walnut kernels
1 teaspoon Worcestershire sauce
salt and pepper

Drain pear halves and arrange on lettuce leaves. Sieve cottage cheese and mix with very finely chopped onion, roughly broken walnuts, Worcestershire sauce, salt and pepper to taste. Put some of the mixture in each pear half. Garnish with chopped parsley or chives if available.

### PINEAPPLE CHICKEN SALAD

1 lb. cooked chicken
3 sticks celery
12 stuffed olives
1 small pineapple
¼ pint mayonnaise
4 tablespoons chicken stock
salt and pepper
lettuce leaves

Dice the chicken meat and mix with finely chopped celery and sliced olives. Cut the pineapple flesh into dice and mix with the chicken. Thin the mayonnaise with the chicken stock to make a light creamy dressing, and season well with salt and pepper. Serve in individual portions on lettuce leaves.

### PINEAPPLE SHRIMP SALAD

16-oz. can pineapple chunks
8 oz. peeled shrimps
1 small onion
8 oz. cold cooked peas
½ pint mayonnaise
1 teaspoon curry powder

Drain pineapple and cut each chunk in half. Mix with shrimps, shredded onion and peas, and toss in mayonnaise spiced with the curry powder. Serve with a winter salad of endive, watercress and shredded cabbage.

### RASPBERRY SOUP

1 lb. raspberries
4 oz. sugar
2 teaspoons lemon juice
2 oz. butter
2 tablespoons plain flour
¼ teaspoon salt
pinch of ground cinnamon
1 pint milk

Keep a few raspberries for garnishing. Crush the remainder lightly with half the sugar and the lemon juice and chill for 30 minutes. Melt the butter, stir in the flour, salt, cinnamon and remaining sugar. Add the milk and stir over a gentle heat until the mixture begins to thicken. Chill and just before serving, stir in the raspberry mixture. Garnish with the reserved fruit.

### FRUIT AND NUT CHEESE SALAD

2 oz. chopped nuts
3 oz. chopped dates or figs
1 banana
1 eating apple
2 oz. grated cheese
3 tablespoons oil
1 tablespoon vinegar
salt and pepper

Mix together the nuts, dates or figs, sliced banana and apple and grated cheese. Mix the oil and vinegar, season lightly with salt and pepper and pour over the salad.

### CURRY RICE SALAD

2 oz. seedless raisins
8 oz. patna rice
1½ tablespoons curry powder
1 eating apple
juice of ½ lemon
½ pint mayonnaise

Soak raisins in warm water for 1 hour, and drain well. Cook rice in boiling salted water, to which curry powder has been added, for 12 minutes, or until just tender. Drain in a colander, rinse in cold water and drain thoroughly again. Mix rice and raisins. Cut apple into small chunks, leaving skin on, and dip into lemon juice. Add to rice and raisin mixture. Stir remaining lemon juice into mayonnaise, and use to bind rice mixture.

### FRUIT AND RICE SALAD

8 oz. patna rice
8 oz. tongue cut in a thick slice
8-oz. tin pear halves
8-oz. tin pineapple chunks
juice of 1 lemon
1 head of lettuce

Cook rice in boiling salted water, drain in colander, rinse in cold water and drain thoroughly again. Cut tongue into small cubes. Drain pears and pineapple, and cut both fruit into small neat pieces. Toss tongue, pears and pineapple with rice and lemon juice, and arrange on lettuce leaves.

### COCKTAIL STICKS

melon or pineapple
prawns, cheese or ham

Cut melon or fresh pineapple into cubes, or use canned pineapple. Alternate fruit cubes on cocktail sticks with prawns, cubes of firm cheese or cooked ham. If preferred, thin slices of ham can be wrapped round the fruit cubes and speared on sticks. Cherries and stuffed olives may also be used here and there on the sticks.

# (4)

# Main Courses and Accompaniments

The combination of meat, fish and poultry with fruit is sometimes dismissed as a new-fangled foreign notion, but in fact the sharpness of fruit has been combined with the richness of many savoury dishes for centuries in the European kitchen. We have now become all too sadly familiar with the cliché of a slice of canned pineapple with grilled ham, or of a peach half-stuffed with cottage cheese on a wilting lettuce leaf, but we should not be deterred from more exciting experiments. Fruit may be used as a stuffing, a grilled accompaniment or a side salad, or as an integral part of a recipe. It is particularly refreshing with rich pork, duck and goose, ham and sausages.

### FRUITED HADDOCK

4 haddock steaks
tabasco
paprika
1 grapefruit

Lightly grease the base of a grill pan. Place fish on pan and sprinkle with salt and a few drops of tabasco and paprika pepper. Grill for six minutes, then cover fish with peeled and pithed grapefruit sections and continue grilling for a further four minutes or longer if steaks are thick.

### HADDOCK WITH GRAPES

1½ lb. haddock
1 oz. butter
1 oz. plain flour
fish stock or water
3 tablespoons double cream
4 oz. seedless grapes
seasoning

Skin fish and divide into four portions. Poach in stock or

water. Make a sauce using the butter, flour and ½ pint of cooking liquid. Add 2 tablespoons cream and peeled grapes. Adjust seasoning. Pour over fish. Dribble remaining cream on top and place under a hot grill to glaze.

### HALIBUT WITH BANANAS

2 lb. halibut fillets
1 oz. plain flour
1 egg
2 oz. fine breadcrumbs
2 bananas
2 oz. butter
2 oz. toasted flaked almonds

Cut the fish into small portions, and roll in flour, beaten egg and breadcrumbs. Fry in deep fat until golden brown, drain and put on to a warm serving dish with slices of uncooked banana. Heat the butter until frothing and pour over the fish. Sprinkle with almonds.

### MACKEREL WITH ORANGE

4 medium-sized mackerel
8 tablespoons oil
5 tablespoons white wine
few drops tabasco
salt and freshly ground black pepper
2 oz. black olives
2 oranges
fresh bay leaves

Clean, gut and wash the mackerel and remove the heads. Make two slanting incisions with a sharp knife across both sides of each fish. Lay the mackerel in the grill pan and pour over the mixed oil, wine and seasonings. Leave the fish in the marinade for two hours, turning occasionally. Place pan under pre-heated grill and cook the fish for 5-8 minutes on each side, depending on thickness. When cooked, lift the mackerel carefully on to a serving dish. Pour over juices from the pan and when fish is quite cold, garnish with olives, peeled orange rings and bay leaves. Serve with green salad, and brown bread and butter.

### COMPANY CHICKEN

2 oz. butter
1 medium onion
4 oz. cooked ham
1 teaspoon curry powder
1 tablespoon flour
4 oz. button mushrooms
¾ pint chicken stock
¼ pint thin cream or top of milk
2 tablespoons lemon juice
1 tablespoon salt
1 lb. cooked chicken
1 small can pear halves
boiled rice

Melt butter and gently cook chopped onion and ham until golden. Stir in curry powder, flour, whole mushrooms, stock and cream and simmer very gently for 10 minutes. Stir in lemon juice and salt, and taste for seasoning, then add chicken cut in small pieces and pears cut in large cubes. Simmer for 10 minutes, then serve over hot boiled rice.

### FRUITED ROAST DUCK

4½-5 lb. duck
1 onion
½ oz. butter
6 oz. cooking apples
4 oz. soaked prunes
1 large orange
2 eating apples

Prick the duck through skin and fat with a fork. Rub inside and out with salt. Chop the onion and fry it in the butter until soft. Chop the cooking apples and add to the fat. Reserve 4 prunes; stone the rest, chop them and stir into the pan until hot. Stuff the bird with this mixture, and stand on a rack in a baking tin. Roast at 450°F (Gas Mark 8) for

30 minutes, then reduce to 350°F (Gas Mark 4) for 1 hour. Half an hour before the end of cooking time, cut the eating apples in half, remove the cores and replace each with a stoned prune. Put into the cooking fat, cut sides down, turn over and put into oven. After 15 minutes, take duck from rack, pour off all the fat, and put the bird into the tin. Pour the orange juice and grated rind over it. At serving time, put the duck on to a heated dish and garnish with the stuffed apples.

### SWEDISH ROAST GOOSE

10-12 lb. goose
1 tablespoon salt
½ teaspoon pepper
6 eating apples
20 prunes
1 pint beef stock

Rub the bird inside and out with the salt and pepper. Peel and quarter the apples, and stone the prunes. Stuff the goose with the apples and prunes. Roast at 425°F (Gas Mark 7) for 2 hours, basting frequently with beef stock. When almost done, baste with 2 tablespoons cold water to make the skin brittle, and leave the oven door slightly open. Strain the pan juices and remove fat. If liked, thicken the juices slightly to make gravy. Serve with red cabbage and apple sauce.

### NORMANDY PHEASANT

1 pheasant
4 oz. butter
1¼ lb. peeled and sliced apples
6 tablespoons thin cream

Season the pheasant, and brown in butter. Line a casserole with half the apples. Pour over a little of the butter, put in the pheasant and surround with the remaining apples. Pour over the rest of the butter and stir in cream. Cover tightly and cook at 350°F (Gas Mark 4) for 45 minutes.

AUTUMN RABBIT

1 rabbit, jointed
1 oz. dripping
1 oz. plain flour
½ bottle red wine
1 onion
1 carrot
2 oz. mushrooms
1 garlic clove
thyme, parsley and bay leaf
1 orange
4 oz. grapes
2 eating apples
salt and pepper

Clean and wipe rabbit joints and fry them in the dripping until golden. Remove rabbit to a casserole. Work the flour into the fat in the pan and gradually add the wine. Simmer for 3 minutes, and pour over the rabbit. Add sliced onion, carrot, mushrooms, crushed garlic and herbs. Peel the orange, remove pips and slice fruit. Peel grapes and remove pips. Peel, core and slice apples. Put all the fruit into the casserole, and season with plenty of salt and pepper. Cover and cook at 350°F (Gas Mark 4) for 2 hours.

PORK AND APPLE CASSEROLE

1 oz. dripping
2 small onions
12 oz. cooking apples
1½ lb. pork loin chops
1 oz. plain flour
¾ pint stock
salt and pepper
½ teaspoon made mustard
4 whole cloves

Melt the dripping in a frying pan. Slice the onions and peeled apples in rings and fry gently until soft but not brown. Take out of the pan and keep warm. Fry the chops on both sides until brown, and then take out and keep warm. Blend the flour into the fat in the pan and stir until well browned. Stir in the stock and bring to the boil, stirring all the time. Add the salt, pepper, mustard and cloves. Put the chops into a casserole, cover with the apples and onions. Pour over the gravy and put on a lid. Cook at 325°F (Gas Mark 3) for 1½ hours. Serve with jacket or mashed potatoes and a green vegetable.

### CRANBERRY PORK CHOPS

4 pork chops
salt and pepper
8 oz. cranberries
4 oz. honey
2 tablespoons water

Brown the chops on both sides, season with salt and pepper and put into a casserole. Crush the cranberries, mix with the honey and water and pour over the chops. Cover and bake at 350°F (Gas Mark 4) for 1 hour.

### FRUITED PORK CHOPS

4 pork chops
4 oz. raisins
2 oz. dried apricots
juice of 4 oranges
¼ teaspoon curry powder
1 teaspoon salt

Brown chops on both sides in a heavy pan. Add raisins and apricots cut in quarters. Combine juice of oranges with curry powder and salt, and pour over chops. Cover and cook over very low heat for 1 hour, or bake at 350°F (Gas Mark 4) for 1 hour. Be sure there is enough juice, or a little water, to prevent chops burning, but the finished dish should have just enough sauce to coat the chops and fruit. Serve with plainly boiled potatoes.

### PORK AND PEACHES

4 lb. leg of pork
2 cloves unpeeled garlic
2 oranges
salt and pepper
1 large can peach halves

Put pork in a roasting pan, tucking the garlic cloves under the joint. Sprinkle with salt and pepper and add ⅓ pint water. Bake at 425°F (Gas Mark 7) for 10 minutes, then reduce heat to 375°F (Gas Mark 5) and cook for 30 minutes per lb. Half an hour before serving time, take off any surplus fat, and grate peel of 1 orange over joint. Add the juice of 2 oranges to the liquid round the joint, and arrange the drained peach halves in the roasting tin. Finish cooking for 30 minutes, and serve meat surrounded by peaches, with the gravy from the tin.

### APRICOT PORK CHOPS

6 pork chops
1 onion
1 oz. butter
1 tablespoon flour
16-oz. can apricot halves
2 tablespoons tomato purée
1 orange
2 bay leaves
3-4 tablespoons vinegar
salt and pepper
parsley

Trim chops if necessary and remove rind. Fry in hot butter until just brown. Place in a shallow casserole or heatproof dish. Peel and chop the onion and fry in fat in pan. Stir in flour. Remove from the heat. Reserve six apricots for garnish and sieve the rest to form a purée. Stir into the pan with the tomato purée, grated orange rind, bay leaves, vinegar and seasoning to taste. Bring to boil, stirring, and cook for 1-2 minutes. Pour over chops. Cover and bake at 400°F (Gas Mark 6) for 40 minutes. Remove pith from orange and slice. Garnish chops with orange slices, apricots and parsley sprigs.

### APRICOT POT ROAST

3 tablespoons lard
4 lb. rolled beef brisket
2 medium onions
¼ teaspoon ground cloves

1 teaspoon salt
½ teaspoon pepper
1 tablespoon brown sugar
½ pint dry cider
16-oz. can apricot halves

Heat lard in a heavy pan, and brown the brisket on all sides. Add sliced onions and cook gently until golden. Add cloves, salt, pepper and sugar and enough water to come halfway up the pan. Cover tightly and simmer for 2½ hours, adding a little cider if liquid begins to dry up. Add remaining cider and drained apricots and continue simmering for 30 minutes. Skim off fat and put meat on serving dish surrounded by apricots. Serve with gravy from the pan.

### HONEY LAMB

2 lb. lean shoulder of lamb
2 oz. butter
2 medium onions
1 clove garlic
8 oz. dried apricots
salt and pepper
2 level tablespoons curry powder
3 tablespoons malt vinegar
10 level tablespoons honey
4 tablespoons white wine

Cut meat in 1 in. cubes. Melt butter in a heavy pan, add chopped onions and crushed garlic and cook until soft and golden. Add apricots which have been cooked in a little water and sieved with their cooking liquid, salt and pepper to taste, curry powder, vinegar and honey, and simmer for 10 minutes. Add wine, then pour mixture over meat in a bowl and leave overnight. Remove meat from the sauce, and thread cubes on skewers. Grill for 15 minutes at medium heat, turning frequently until meat is browned. Serve with the sauce which has been heated and with boiled or fried rice. This is a perfect buffet dish.

ORANGE STUFFED BREAST OF LAMB

4 oz. white breadcrumbs
2 tablespoons chopped parsley
grated rind of 1 orange
half the juice of 1 orange
1 beaten egg
salt and pepper
2 boned breasts of lamb
1 oz. seasoned flour
1 oz. dripping

*Gravy:*
½ oz. flour
1 beef cube in ½ pint hot water
remaining juice of 1 orange
1 tablespoon redcurrant jelly

Prepare stuffing: mix together breadcrumbs, chopped parsley, orange rind and juice and bind with sufficient beaten egg to hold it together. Season and lay half of it on the first breast of lamb. Lay second breast on top and cover with the remaining stuffing. Roll it tightly and tie with string. Roll in seasoned flour and roast in melted dripping for 1 hour at 350°F (Gas Mark 4). At end of cooking time serve breast on a plate. Blend the flour into the fat in the roasting tin, add beef extract stock, orange juice and redcurrant jelly, cook for 2 minutes, and hand separately.

COLLAR BACON WITH PINEAPPLE

3-4 lb. collar bacon
8-oz. tin pineapple slices
cloves
1 level teaspoon mustard
4 oz. brown sugar

✓ sauce may become caramelised

Soak the collar for a few hours. Place in a pan of cold water, bring to the boil and simmer for 1 hour. Remove from pan and strip off the rind. With a sharp knife, score the fat criss-cross. Decorate with rows of small segments of pineapple, each secured with a clove. In a small saucepan, mix together the mustard, brown sugar and pineapple juice to make a sauce. Place the bacon in a baking tin and over it pour the sauce. Bake at 425°F (Gas Mark 7) for 40 minutes, basting occasionally with the sauce. The remainder of the pineapple slices may be heated through and placed around the bacon on the dish. Serve with buttered potatoes and green peas. 220°C

### BACON AND APPLE ROLL

8-12 oz. cold cooked bacon
1 peeled and cored cooking apple
2 oz. fresh breadcrumbs
2 teaspoons chopped parsley
1 teaspoon sage
salt and pepper
1 egg
tomato sauce or gravy
flour
12 oz. puff pastry

Mince the bacon and the apple. Add the crumbs, parsley, sage, salt and pepper and the egg. If necessary, add a little sauce or gravy to bind the ingredients together. Form into a roll, using a little flour, and wrap in thinly rolled puff or flaky pastry. Bake at 425°F (Gas Mark 7) for 35 minutes.

### SAUSAGE AND FRUIT FRY

½ oz. fat
1 lb. pork sausages
4 tablespoons white wine
1 lb. peeled and cored cooking apples
3 peeled and cored pears
3 peeled tomatoes
salt and pepper

Melt the fat in a frying pan and fry the sausages gently until nicely browned all over—about 20 minutes. Remove from the pan and keep warm. Pour the wine into the hot fat, then slice the apples thickly and add to the pan with the thickly sliced pears and quartered tomatoes. Season well with salt and pepper, bring to simmering point, cover the pan and cook very gently for 10 minutes. Arrange this mixture on a serving dish, lay the sausages on top and serve hot.

### APPLE SAVOURY PIE

8 oz. cold roast pork
1½ lb. eating apples
salt and pepper

pinch of ground ginger
¼ pint light ale
8 oz. puff pastry

Dice the meat and slice the peeled apples. Put them into a pie dish in layers, seasoning each meat layer with salt, pepper and ginger. Cover with the ale and put on a pastry lid. Bake at 425°F (Gas Mark 7) for 45 minutes and serve very hot.

### APRICOT SAUSAGE CAKES

1 lb. pork sausage meat
2 oz. breadcrumbs
16-oz. can apricot halves
1 egg
pinch of sage
salt and pepper

Mix the sausage meat and breadcrumbs. Drain the apricot halves and reserve half of them. Chop the rest and mix with the meat, then bind with the egg, and season with sage, salt and pepper to taste. Make into small flat cakes and put on greased baking sheet. Bake at 350°F (Gas Mark 4) for 30 minutes. Top each cake with an apricot half, and continue baking for 10 minutes. Serve with chunks of raw celery and with grated carrots dressed with salt, pepper and lemon juice.

### SAUSAGE AND APPLE LOAF

12 oz. pork sausage meat
2 oz. breadcrumbs
2 eating apples
1 egg
salt and pepper
3 fresh sage leaves

Mix together the sausage meat and breadcrumbs. Mix with grated apple and beaten egg. Season with salt and pepper and add the chopped sage leaves. Put into a loaf tin or a casserole and bake at 350°F (Gas Mark 4) for 1 hour.

### APPLE SAUSAGES

1 lb. fat pork
1 lb. sour apples
paprika

Mince together the pork and peeled apples and flavour lightly with paprika. Form into small sausage shapes or flat cakes and fry. Serve with mashed potatoes.

### BOHEMIAN APPLES

8 oz. fresh breadcrumbs
1 lb. eating apples
1 lb. cold pork or beef
salt and pepper
2 oz. dripping

Put half the breadcrumbs in a buttered baking dish. Put on a layer of peeled and chopped apples, and then of minced meat, seasoning with salt and pepper. Top with remaining breadcrumbs and dot with dripping. Bake at 350°F (Gas Mark 4) for 1 hour. Serve hot with a good brown gravy and horseradish sauce.

### VICTORIAN STUFFED APPLES

4 crisp eating apples
8 oz. cold pork or duck
salt and pepper
3 fresh sage leaves
1 oz. butter
2 oz. fresh breadcrumbs

Core the apples and fill them with minced meat seasoned with salt and pepper and with chopped sage. Dot with butter and bake at 375°F (Gas Mark 5) for 15 minutes. Top with breadcrumbs and continue cooking for 15 minutes.

### CHEESE AND APPLE CHARLOTTE

3 large eating apples
4 oz. butter
8 oz. fine breadcrumbs
8 oz. grated Cheddar cheese
pepper and salt
½ teaspoon made mustard

Peel the apples and grate them finely. Melt the butter and stir in breadcrumbs, apple, seasonings and 6 oz. of the cheese, until the crumbs and apple are just coated with butter and cheese. Put mixture in a greased pie dish and sprinkle with remaining cheese. Bake at 350°F (Gas Mark 4) for 45 minutes. Serve sprinkled with a little chopped parsley and with grilled tomatoes or a salad.

### RASPBERRY SALAD

8 oz. raspberries
4 tablespoons oil
2 tablespoons lemon juice
pinch of sugar
lettuce leaves

Put the raspberries in a bowl and pour over the oil mixed with lemon juice and a little sugar. Lift out the raspberries and arrange on lettuce leaves on individual plates. Serve with roast chicken.

### ORANGE AND ONION SALAD

4 oranges
2 small onions
lettuce leaves
fresh mint

Peel the oranges and slice them crosswise very thinly. Slice the onions and separate into rings. Arrange the orange slices on a bed of lettuce (or of chicory in the winter). Top with onion rings and sprinkle with finely chopped mint. Serve with roast or cold duck.

### PLUM SALAD

1 lb. ripe plums
6 tablespoons oil
2 tablespoons wine vinegar
tarragon

Split the plums and remove the stones. Mix the oil and vinegar and pour over the plums. Garnish with tarragon and serve well chilled with chicken or roast beef.

### PINEAPPLE COLESLAW

1 lb. firm white cabbage
3 sticks celery
1 small pineapple
¼ pint mayonnaise
salt, pepper and mustard powder

Shred the cabbage very finely and mix with the finely chopped celery and shredded pineapple. Season the mayonnaise highly with salt, pepper and mustard to taste, and stir in the cabbage, celery and pineapple. This is crisp and refreshing but filling, and is excellent for a buffet meal.

### PRUNE AND SAUSAGE STUFFING

1 tablespoon oil
1 small chopped onion
2 oz. sliced mushrooms
8 oz. sausage meat
4 oz. prunes
2 oz. fresh white breadcrumbs
pinch of sage
salt and pepper

Heat oil and fry onion and mushrooms for a few minutes. Mix together sausage meat, chopped plumped (soaked) prunes, breadcrumbs, sage and seasoning. Add the onion and mushrooms and mix all well.

### APPLE AND SOUR CREAM STUFFING

3 peeled and chopped dessert apples
2 chopped onions
2 tablespoons oil
4 oz. fresh white breadcrumbs
1 teaspoon sage
1 teaspoon lemon juice
3 dessertspoons sour cream or yoghurt
salt and pepper

Sauté apple and onion in oil. Add breadcrumbs, sage and lemon juice; moisten with sour cream or yoghurt and season to taste.

RAISIN AND APPLE STUFFING

2 peeled chopped dessert apples
4 oz. fresh white breadcrumbs
2 oz. chopped raisins
2 oz. chopped hazelnuts
1 teaspoon made mustard
2 tablespoons golden syrup
1 dessertspoon oil
lemon juice
salt and pepper

Mix together apple, breadcrumbs, raisins, hazelnuts and mustard. Heat syrup and oil and use to moisten the dry ingredients. Add lemon juice, salt and pepper to taste.

APPLE STUFFING

8 oz. cooking apples
2 oz. breadcrumbs
4 fresh sage leaves
2 shallots
shake of cayenne pepper

Peel and core the apples and cut them into slices. Simmer in 4 tablespoons water until soft and mix with breadcrumbs, chopped sage and shallots, and pepper. Use for pork, duck or goose.

CRANBERRY STUFFING

12 oz. cranberries
6 oz. sugar
1 large white loaf
6 oz. melted butter
8 oz. raisins
1 tablespoon salt
½ teaspoon ground cinnamon
grated rind of 2 lemons

Chop the cranberries and mix them with the sugar. Remove the crusts from the bread (use it when the loaf is at least 24 hours old) and cut the bread into small cubes. Toss these in the melted butter and mix with the cranberries and sugar.

Add the raisins, salt, cinnamon and lemon rind and mix with ⅓ pint water. Mix very thoroughly and stuff a joint or bird.

This is enough for an 8 lb. turkey, and the quantity can be halved for a 4 lb. joint of pork.

GOOSEBERRY SAUCE

2 lb. gooseberries
6 oz. Demerara sugar
1½ oz. butter

Cook the topped and tailed gooseberries in ½ pint water with the sugar until soft. Put through a sieve and reheat gently. Just before serving, stir in flakes of butter.

GOOSEBERRY SAUCE (for mackerel)

1 oz. butter
¾ oz. plain flour
8 oz. gooseberries
salt, pepper and sugar
½ oz. butter

Melt the butter and stir in the flour. Cook gently until light brown. Gently stir in ¾ pint water to make a smooth thin sauce. Add the topped and tailed gooseberries, salt and pepper and a pinch of sugar and simmer until the berries are soft. Put through a sieve and reheat, adding the butter just before serving.

SPANISH SAUCE (for salmon)

½ pint white wine vinegar
4 oz. apple slices
1 saltspoon cayenne pepper
pinch of paprika

Boil the vinegar until reduced to half quantity. Put in the apple slices, pepper and paprika and cook gently, stirring well, until the mixture is a smooth purée.

CRANBERRY SAUCE

12 oz. cranberries
12 oz. sugar

Wash the cranberries and cook with ¾ pint water and sugar for ten minutes. Skim and cool and serve with meat or poultry.

BAKED CRANBERRIES

8 oz. cranberries
12 oz. sugar

Wash the cranberries and put them into a baking dish with the sugar. Cover and bake at 350°F (Gas Mark 4) for 1 hour. Serve with meat or poultry.

CRANBERRY RELISH

2 large oranges
2 eating apples
1 lb. cranberries
1 lb. sugar

Peel the oranges, keeping the peel from half the fruit. Chop the flesh finely. Mince the reserved peel coarsely with the unpeeled apples and the cranberries. Mix with the orange flesh and sugar and chill for 8 hours before serving with meat or poultry.

GRILLED PEACHES

4 fresh peaches
melted butter
sugar
cinnamon

Peel the peaches and cut them in half. Brush with melted butter and sprinkle with sugar and cinnamon. Grill and serve with kidneys, pork or ham.

Canned peaches may be used, but fresh ones have a sharper flavour and better texture to serve as an accompaniment to meat.

GRILLED PINEAPPLE

1 small fresh pineapple
2 oz. brown or white sugar
2 oz. butter

Peel the pineapple and cut into thick rings. Sprinkle well with sugar and dot with flakes of butter. Grill to a toffee brown, basting with melted butter. Serve with ham or turkey.

BAKED ORANGES

8 oranges
4 oz. sugar
4 tablespoons butter

Wash the oranges and grate the skins slightly. Cover with water and boil for 30 minutes. Drain and cool, then cut a slice from the stem end of each orange and remove the core. Put sugar and butter into each orange, and stand them in a baking tin with 1 in. water. Cover and bake at 325°F (Gas Mark 3) for 1½ hours until the skins are tender. Serve with turkey, ham, pork or veal.

(5)

# Hot Puddings

Hot fruit can be delicious but it can also be very boring. There is nothing more deadly and unappetising than fruit stewed in a mass of water, sweetened with sugar at random. On the other hand, apples, plums and apricots are superb if cooked in the oven in a casserole without liquid but with a knob of butter and either sugar or honey for sweetening. The addition of a complementary spirit or liqueur such as rum, or apricot brandy, creates ambrosia. Pears and peaches are delicious if cooked in the oven with a little wine and sugar (red for pears, white for peaches); the exotic quince is perfect in cider, and the humble rhubarb needs no addition but some jam or marmalade and a little extra sweetening—but no water at all.

Suet puddings and shortcrust pies are familiar hot fruit dishes, but it is worth treating fruit in more exciting ways with the addition of spices, plenty of butter and brown sugar, a dash of orange or lemon juice.

While the following recipes specify the preferred fruit for a dish, different fruits may be used according to season, or a combination of fruits. Many fruits pair naturally together and complement each other. Try apples with apricots or quinces; bananas with oranges; blackberries with apples or pears; oranges with cranberries or quinces; peaches with raspberries; plums with oranges; and rhubarb with raspberries or oranges.

### APPLE BUTTERSCOTCH

2 tablespoons butter
3 tablespoons golden syrup
1 tablespoon brown sugar
1 lb. eating apples
4 thin bread slices

Put the butter, syrup and sugar into a frying pan and cook gently until just turning colour. Peel and slice the apples and add to the toffee mixture, turning them over and over until cooked. Take out the apples and keep them. Put the bread into the toffee mixture and turn until they have absorbed all the liquid. Put the bread into a lightly greased serving dish, top with apples, and serve with cream.

### APPLE HONEY CHARLOTTE

1 oz. butter
4 oz. fresh white breadcrumbs
1 lb. cooking apples
½ lemon
4 oz. honey
1 tablespoon water

Use the butter to grease a pie dish thickly. Press a layer of breadcrumbs on to bottom and sides. Peel, core and slice apples thinly, and arrange alternate layers of apples and crumbs in the dish, finishing with crumbs. Grate rind from the lemon, and squeeze out the juice. Put lemon rind, juice, honey and water in a saucepan, and bring to the boil, stirring until well blended. Pour over the apples and crumbs, and bake at 325°F (Gas Mark 3) for 1¼ hours. Serve with cream or custard. 160°C

### APPLE SOUFFLÉ OMELETTE

2 eggs
1 teaspoon caster sugar
¼ teaspoon vanilla essence
1 dessert apple
2 tablespoons honey
½ oz. butter

Separate eggs and beat up yolks with caster sugar and essence. Peel the apple, remove core and cut apple into thin slices. Put in a saucepan with honey, heat gently and keep warm. Whisk egg whites until stiff, and fold in yolk mixture. Melt butter in 6 in. omelette pan, and pour in the egg mixture. Cook over gentle heat until just set. Colour the top lightly under grill. Put apple and honey mixture on one half of the omelette, fold over and serve on a hot plate, sprinkled with a little sugar. This is enough for two servings.

### DUTCH APPLE PUDDING

8 oz. self-raising flour
pinch of salt
4 oz. shredded suet
1½ lb. cooking apples
4 oz. sugar
juice of 1 lemon
2 tablespoons golden syrup
1 oz. soft brown sugar

Mix the flour, salt and suet together and add enough cold water to make a firm dough. Roll out thinly and line a square tin with half the dough. Peel the apples and cut them in slices. Arrange on the dough and sprinkle with sugar and lemon juice. Cover with the other half of the dough and seal edges with a little water. Spread with golden syrup and sprinkle with brown sugar. Bake at 350°F (Gas Mark 4) for 1 hour until the crust is crisp like toffee.

### LORD JEFFREY AMHERST PUDDING

8 large ½-in. slices of bread
3 oz. butter
1½ lb. eating apples
6 oz. brown sugar
1 teaspoon ground cinnamon
1 teaspoon ground cloves
½ teaspoon salt

Spread the bread slices with butter and cut each slice into three pieces. Line an ovenware dish with buttered slices. Peel, core and slice the apples. Sprinkle generously with most of the brown sugar, cinnamon, cloves and all the salt. Put the apples into the dish and top with the remaining slices, buttered side up. Sprinkle with remaining sugar and spice. Cover the dish and bake at 300°F (Gas Mark 2) for 1½ hours. Remove lid and continue cooking for 30 minutes. Turn out and serve with brandy butter.

### APPLE BIRDS' NESTS

6 eating apples
5 teaspoons plain flour
1 teaspoon salt
¾ pint milk
3 eggs

Peel and core apples and put in a large buttered baking dish. Make a paste with flour, salt, and just enough milk to moisten the flour. Add beaten egg yolks and stir until smooth. Fold in stiffly whisked whites and rest of the milk. Pour mixture over apples and bake at 325°F (Gas Mark 3) for 1 hour. Serve very hot with melted apricot jam as a sauce.

### TOP OF THE STOVE APPLE PIE

1 lb. cooking apples
2 cloves
1 tablespoon lemon juice
4 oz. sugar
¼ pint water
1 oz. butter
1 dessertspoon semolina
2 eggs
8 oz. shortbread triangles
2 tablespoons extra sugar
2 tablespoons chopped nuts

Cook the apples, peeled, cored and sliced, with the cloves, lemon juice, sugar and water until soft. Remove cloves, whip in butter and semolina and bring to boil, stirring. Sweeten to taste. Cool a little and beat in egg yolks and cook gently, without boiling, for 1 minute. Pour into a pie plate and arrange shortbread around the dish. Whisk egg whites and gradually add extra sugar. Beat over boiling water until thick and creamy. Fold half the nuts into the meringue and pile over the apple filling. Sprinkle with remaining nuts.

### APPLE CRISP

6 cooking apples
1 tablespoon lemon juice
1½ oz. plain flour
3 oz. porridge oats
4 oz. brown sugar
½ level teaspoon salt
1 level teaspoon cinnamon
2 oz. melted butter

Peel, core and slice the apples and place in a greased shallow baking dish. Sprinkle with lemon juice. Combine the dry ingredients, add melted butter and mix until crumbly. Sprinkle crumb mixture on top of apples, bake at 350°F (Gas Mark 4) for about 30 minutes, or until the apples are tender. Serve hot with cream or custard. 180°C

### APPLE SLICES WITH HONEY ✓ v. quick to do. OK in oven

4 cooking apples
2 oz. butter
1 tablespoon honey OK with golden syrup
¼ pint whipped cream
pinch of cinnamon don't make too sweet

Core and slice apples ½ in. thick. Cover one side of each slice with a layer of butter and put in buttered pan, butter side down. Spread honey on top, and put under grill for 7 minutes. Serve with cream whipped with cinnamon.

### APRICOT APPLE PIE

1 lb. shortcrust pastry
1½ lb. cooking apples
1½ tablespoons lemon juice
4 oz. granulated sugar
3 oz. soft brown sugar
3 tablespoons plain flour
1 teaspoon cinnamon
½ teaspoon nutmeg
¼ teaspoon salt
1-lb. can apricot halves
1 teaspoon vanilla essence
½ teaspoon almond essence
2 tablespoons butter

Line a pie dish with half the pastry. Peel apples and slice thinly, and toss in lemon juice. Mix the granulated and brown sugars, flour, cinnamon, nutmeg and salt and toss the apple slices in this mixture, then arrange in pastry case. Put apricot halves, cut side down on top of the apples. Sprinkle with vanilla and almond essences and dot with butter. Cover with remaining pastry, and bake at 400°F

(Gas Mark 6) for 20 minutes, then reduce heat to 350° (Gas Mark 4) and continue cooking for 25 minutes.

APRICOT FOUR-DECKER

16-oz. can apricot halves
1 lb. shortcrust pastry
2 oz. sugar
1 oz. butter
pinch of mixed spice

Drain the apricots well (save the syrup for sweetening another dish). Divide the pastry into four pieces and roll each piece out thinly to fit a 7 in. sponge sandwich tin or square tin. Grease the tin and put in one sheet of pastry. Arrange one-third of the fruit on top. Sprinkle with a little sugar, and put on one or two flakes of butter and a sprinkle of spice. Put on another layer of pastry, and then fruit, sugar, butter and spice. Continue in layers, ending with pastry and press down edges well. Bake at 425°F (Gas Mark 7) for 35 minutes. Serve hot with plenty of thick cream.

This is a traditional Westmorland pie, and can also be made with apples, rhubarb, gooseberries, blackcurrants or any other fruit in season. Cut the fruit up finely, and use about 6 oz. sugar to 1 lb. raw fruit, according to tartness. A little more butter may also be added when raw fruit is used, and the spice may be varied. Nutmeg, cinnamon or ginger can be used separately, or mixed together. A creamy egg custard is good instead of cream to accompany the pie.

APRICOT TURNOVERS

16-oz. can apricot halves
8 oz. plain flour
pinch of salt
½-1 teaspoon ground cinnamon
5 oz. butter
granulated sugar

Drain juice from apricots and chop fruit. Sift flour, salt and half the cinnamon. Cut 4 oz. butter into pieces and rub into flour until like breadcrumbs. Mix to a soft, not sticky, dough with some of the syrup from the apricots. Divide into eight and roll each piece out to a 6-inch round. Trim edges. Brush with water. Divide chopped apricots between pastry rounds. Sprinkle with remaining cinnamon and a few flakes of butter. Fold in half. Pinch edges together. Brush with remaining apricot syrup and sprinkle with sugar. Bake at 425°F (Gas Mark 7) for 20 minutes.

APRICOT FRITTERS

2 oz. plain flour
1 dessertspoon sugar
½ teaspoon baking powder
½ teaspoon salt
1 egg
2½ fl. oz. milk
1 teaspoon salad oil
1 teaspoon grated lemon peel
1 lb. 12 oz.-can apricot halves
oil for deep frying

Sift flour with sugar, baking powder and salt, and gradually work in egg, milk, salad oil and lemon peel. Drain apricots very thoroughly and dry them on paper towels. Heat frying oil to 375°F. Roll apricot halves lightly in flour, shake off excess, then dip in batter, coating evenly. Deep-fry a few at a time, turning once, for 3 or 4 minutes until golden. Drain on paper towels and serve hot with whipped cream slightly sweetened and flavoured with a little almond essence.

APRICOT LAYER PUDDING

4 tablespoons warm golden syrup
8 oz. self-raising flour
½ teaspoon salt
½ teaspoon baking powder
½ teaspoon bicarbonate of soda
4 oz. shredded suet
1 oz. caster sugar
few drops almond essence
16-oz. can apricot halves
apricot jam

Lightly grease a quart pudding basin and cover bottom with 1 tablespoon syrup. Sift flour, salt and baking powder and bicarbonate of soda. Add suet and sugar and almond essence, and mix to a paste with a little syrup from the can of apricots. Divide pastry into three pieces and roll into rounds to fit basin. Put a layer of apricots in basin, cut side down, then a round of pastry. Continue layers of syrup, apricots and pastry, finishing with pastry. Cover with foil and steam 2½ hours. Turn out on warm dish and serve with apricot jam heated and thinned with a little water.

### APRICOT SOUFFLÉ

16-oz. can apricot halves  OK with fresh apricots
4 oz. sugar
1 teaspoon lemon juice
5 egg whites
1 oz. ground almonds or hazelnuts

Mash the drained apricots, and put through a sieve. Add sugar and cook over low heat until sugar is melted, stirring well. Add lemon juice and leave until cool. Beat egg whites until stiff but not dry, and fold into apricot mixture. Put into a buttered and sugared soufflé dish, sprinkle with nuts and bake at 325°F (Gas Mark 3) for 40 minutes.
160°C

### BANANAS IN ORANGE SAUCE

6 bananas
3 oranges
1 oz. butter
2 oz. brown sugar

Peel the bananas and cut in thick slices. Grate the rind from 1 orange and work into the butter and sugar. Peel the oranges and cut into thin crosswise slices, removing the pips. Arrange in layers in an ovenware dish with bananas and pieces of orange butter, finishing with bananas. Dot with any remaining orange butter. Bake at 400°F (Gas Mark 6) for 10 minutes. Serve very hot. A little rum worked into the orange butter enhances the flavour. 200°C

### BLACKBERRY PANCAKES

4 oz. plain flour
2 tablespoons sugar

1 egg
½ pint milk
8 oz. blackberries
1 tablespoon melted butter

Blend together the flour, sugar, egg yolk, milk and blackberries to make a smooth batter. Add the butter and fold in the stiffly beaten egg white. Fry small pancakes in butter, browning on both sides. Serve very hot with vanilla ice cream.

### CRANBERRY SPONGE PUDDING

1 lb. cooking apples
8 oz. cranberries
4 oz. sugar
3 oz. stale spongecake crumbs
2 eggs
4 oz. caster sugar

Peel and cut up apples and simmer with cranberries until pulpy. Add sugar and crumbs and stir well. Cool the mixture, and then beat in the egg yolks. Put into an ovenware dish and bake at 350°F (Gas Mark 4) for 20 minutes until the top is set. Beat the egg whites stiffly, fold in the caster sugar, and pile the meringue on top of the cranberry mixture. Cook for 10 minutes longer, and serve hot.

### GOOSEBERRY AMBER PIE

8 oz. shortcrust pastry
1½ lb. gooseberries
6 oz. caster sugar
1 oz. butter
2 eggs

Line a pie plate with the pastry. Top and tail the fruit and put into a saucepan with 6 tablespoons water. Simmer until softened a little, then add 4 oz. sugar and let it dissolve. Continue simmering until the fruit is completely soft. Cool, and beat in butter and egg yolks. Put into the pastry case. Bake at 375°F (Gas Mark 5) for 35 minutes. Whip the egg whites until stiff and fold in the remaining 2 oz. of sugar. Spread over the fruit and return to the oven for 10 minutes.

GOOSEBERRY TANSY

1 lb. gooseberries
4 oz. butter
2 eggs
¼ pint double cream
3 oz. sugar

Top and tail the gooseberries and put into a pan with the butter and 4 tablespoons of water. Simmer until cooked. Separate the eggs and beat the yolks. Whip the cream lightly and fold in the yolks. Cool the gooseberries, stir in the cream mixture and sweeten with the sugar. Whisk the egg whites stiffly and fold into the mixture. Melt a little butter in an omelette pan and pour in the gooseberry mixture. Cook gently for 5 minutes until the mixture sets and puffs up. Turn on to a hot serving dish and sprinkle with a little caster sugar and lemon juice.

PEACH CRUMBLE PIE

8 oz. puff pastry
2 oz. butter
1½ oz. plain flour
6 oz. caster sugar
16-oz. can peach halves or slices
pinch of nutmeg
pinch of cinnamon

Line a pie plate with the puff pastry. Rub together butter and flour and mix in sugar. Sprinkle half this mixture on the pastry and cover with drained peach halves or slices. Sprinkle with 4 tablespoons juice from peaches and nutmeg and cinnamon. Sprinkle remaining butter and sugar mixture on top of fruit. Bake at 350°F (Gas Mark 4) for 40 minutes. Serve with cream or ice cream.

SCALLOPED PEACHES

16-oz. can peach slices
4 oz. dry white breadcrumbs
2 tablespoons melted butter
½ teaspoon ground cinnamon

Drain peach slices. Mix together crumbs, butter and cinnamon, and sprinkle a layer in a shallow oven dish. Top with peach slices, and sprinkle on remaining crumb mixture. Bake at 350°F (Gas Mark 4) for 25 minutes, then uncover and bake 15 minutes. Serve with thin cream.

### PEACH DUMPLINGS

4 fresh peaches
4 tablespoons butter
4 tablespoons sugar
nutmeg
8 oz. shortcrust pastry
12 oz. soft brown sugar

Peel the peaches by dipping them in boiling water for a minute, and then rubbing off the skins. Take out the stones, leaving the peaches as whole as possible. Fill each cavity with 1 tablespoon butter and 1 tablespoon sugar, and sprinkle with nutmeg. Roll out the pastry about ⅛ in. thick and cut into four squares. Put a peach in the centre of each, make into parcels and seal the edges with a little water. Turn upside down on a deep baking tray.

In a saucepan, heat the sugar with 8 tablespoons water for 5 minutes to make a thick syrup. Spoon some syrup over the dumplings and bake at 425°F (Gas Mark 7) for 10 minutes. Reduce heat to 350°F (Gas Mark 4) and continue baking for 30 minutes, basting with the syrup every ten minutes. Serve warm or cold, with cream.

### FLAMING PEACHES

4 large fresh peaches
2 tablespoons caster sugar
2 tablespoons brandy

Peel peaches, place in warmed dish, cover with sugar and heat gently. When ready, heat the brandy in a spoon, light it and pour over the peaches.

### PEAR UPSIDE-DOWN PUDDING

| *Glaze:* | *Pudding:* |
|---|---|
| 3 oz. butter | 2 oz. butter |
| 6 oz. soft brown sugar | 4 oz. sugar |
| 16-oz. can pear halves | 1 egg |
| | ¼ pint milk |
| | 6 oz. plain flour |
| | 1 teaspoon baking powder |
| | ½ teaspoon salt |

Melt 3 oz. butter in heavy pan and add brown sugar. Stir well and put into 8×8 in. square cake tin. Arrange drained pear halves close together on sugar mixture. Cream 2 oz. butter with sugar and add beaten egg. Add milk alternately with flour sifted with baking powder and salt, and pour pudding mixture over fruit. Bake at 350°F (Gas Mark 4) for 45 minutes. Turn out and serve fruit-side up.

### PEAR AND APRICOT CRISP

1 lb. 12 oz.-can pear halves
1 lb. 12 oz.-can apricot halves
1 large orange
2 oz. Cornflakes
8 oz. sugar
4 oz. melted butter

Drain pears and apricots, and cut fruit in large pieces. Mix fruit in bottom of baking dish. Grate 1 teaspoon orange rind, and squeeze juice from orange. Sprinkle fruit with rind and juice. Crush Cornflakes and mix with sugar and melted butter. Sprinkle over fruit and bake at 350°F (Gas Mark 4) for 30 minutes.

### BAKED PEARS WITH ORANGE SAUCE

1 lb. 12-oz. can pear halves
4 whole cloves
1 in. stick cinnamon
6 slices lemon
6 rounded tablespoons orange marmalade

Drain the pear halves and put cut side down in a shallow baking dish. Simmer the pear syrup with the spices, lemon slices and marmalade for 10 minutes. Pour over the pears and bake at 350°F (Gas Mark 4) for 20 minutes.

### HONEY BAKED PEARS

4 dessert pears
6 oz. honey
4 tablespoons lemon juice
1 teaspoon ground cinnamon
1 oz. butter

Peel the pears, remove cores and cut in half. Arrange in buttered oven dish, cut side up. Blend together honey and lemon juice and pour over pears. Sprinkle with cinnamon and dot with butter. Bake at 350°F (Gas Mark 4) for 20 minutes. Serve hot with cream.

### PEAR TART

8 oz. puff pastry
1 lb. firm eating pears
4 oz. honey
1 egg yolk

Roll pastry into one long strip and divide into two equal rectangles. Peel pears, cut in slices, and poach in a syrup made from honey and 2 tablespoons water until just tender. Cool to lukewarm. Spread pear slices on one piece of pastry, leaving ¾ in. border, and moisten border with a little water. Put on second piece of pastry and press edges together. Mix egg yolk with 1 teaspoon water and brush surface of pastry with this glaze. Bake at 400°F (Gas Mark 6) for 20 minutes. Serve warm with thick cream which may be flavoured with a pinch of cinnamon or a dash of rum or brandy.

### PINEAPPLE PUDDING

3 oz. self-raising flour
pinch of salt
2 oz. shredded suet
1½ oz. butter
1½ oz. soft brown sugar
1 small tin pineapple chunks
arrowroot

Lightly grease 1-pint pudding basin. Sift flour and salt and mix with suet. Mix to a soft dropping consistency with about 3 tablespoons juice from the can of pineapple. Cream butter and sugar together and spread in bottom of pudding basin. Arrange 8 pineapple chunks on this, and cover with suet mixture. Cover with buttered foil and steam for 2 hours. Turn out on to a warm plate and serve with a sauce made from the rest of the pineapple juice thickened with 1 teaspoon arrowroot, adding the remaining chunks cut in small pieces.

### PINEAPPLE UPSIDE-DOWN PUDDING

*Topping:*

8 fresh or canned pineapple rings
3 oz. butter
5 oz. brown sugar
2 oz. chopped walnuts

*Pudding:*

2 oz. butter
4 oz. caster sugar
1 egg
6 oz. plain flour
2 teaspoons baking powder
½ teaspoon salt
4 tablespoons milk

Prepare the fresh pineapple or drain the canned pineapple. Melt the butter and stir in the brown sugar. Pour into an 8 in. square cake tin and arrange the pineapple rings close together. Sprinkle thickly with walnuts. Cream together the butter and sugar and add the egg. Beat in the flour sifted with baking powder and salt, and the milk. Pour on to the pineapple and bake at 350°F (Gas Mark 4) for 45 minutes. Turn out fruit-side up and serve hot with cream.

### GINGERBREAD PLUM PUDDING

1½ lb. yellow plums
7 oz. caster sugar
2 oz. butter
3 oz. black treacle
1 oz. golden syrup
5 tablespoons milk
1 beaten egg
4 oz. plain flour
1 teaspoon ground mixed spice
1 teaspoon ground ginger
½ teaspoon bicarbonate of soda

Wash and drain the plums and mix with 6 oz. sugar. Put into a greased ovenware dish. Warm the butter, black treacle and golden syrup. Remove from the heat and add milk and beaten egg, and leave the mixture to cool. In a bowl, sieve flour, remaining 1 oz. sugar, spices and soda. Add the cooled treacle mixture and mix well together. Pour over the fruit, spreading evenly. Bake at 325°F (Gas Mark 3) for 1¼ hours.

### CINNAMON PLUM TART

4 oz. butter
6 oz. plain flour
10 oz. caster sugar
1 egg yolk
1 tablespoon lemon juice
1½ lb. plums
1 teaspoon ground cinnamon

Rub 3 oz. butter into the flour and stir in 3 oz. sugar. Mix to a dough with the egg yolk, 1 teaspoon lemon juice and 3 tablespoons iced water. Chill the pastry well and roll out to fit a 9 in. pie plate, fluting the edges. Cut the plums in half and remove the stones. Arrange cut side up on the pastry. Mix together the remaining 7 oz. sugar and cinnamon and sprinkle half on the plums. Pour over the remaining lemon juice and dot with the remaining 1 oz. butter. Bake at 350°F (Gas Mark 4) for 40 minutes, and then sprinkle with the remaining cinnamon sugar. Serve with cream.

### HOT RASPBERRY PUDDING

1 lb. raspberries
¼ pint soured cream
2 eggs
1 tablespoon sugar
1 tablespoon plain flour

Put the raspberries in an ovenware dish and bake with a lid on at 350°F (Gas Mark 4) for 15 minutes. Beat up the cream, eggs, sugar and flour. Pour over the fruit and bake at 325°F (Gas Mark 3) for 20 minutes.

### RASPBERRY PIE

8 oz. puff pastry
1 lb. raspberries
6 oz. caster sugar
3 eggs

Line a deep pie plate with the pastry and put in the raspberries mixed with half the sugar. Beat the eggs until foamy, add the remaining sugar and beat until thick and creamy. Pour over the fruit and bake at 375°F (Gas Mark 5) for 30 minutes.

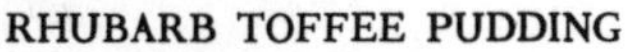

### RHUBARB TOFFEE PUDDING

1 oz. butter
2 oz. soft brown sugar

*Suet Pastry:*
8 oz. self-raising flour
1 teaspoon salt
3 oz. shredded suet
¼ pint water

*Filling:*
1½ lb. young rhubarb
1 oz. chopped candied peel
2 oz. currants
½ lemon
4 oz. sugar
pinch of cinnamon

Butter a 2-pint pudding basin thickly and sprinkle with the brown sugar. Make the suet pastry by sieving together the flour and salt and working in the suet and water. Knead the pastry until it is smooth and cut off one-third for the lid. Line the basin with the larger piece of the pastry. Cut the rhubarb into 1 in. pieces and put half into the basin. Sprinkle in the peel, currants, grated rind and juice of the lemon, half the sugar and the cinnamon. Add the remaining rhubarb and sugar, and pour in 6 tablespoons water. Cover with a lid made from the remaining pastry. Cover with a piece of greased greaseproof paper. Bake at 350°F (Gas Mark 4) for 1¼ hours. Turn out to serve with cream or egg custard.

### RHUBARB SPONGE

2 lb. rhubarb
3 oz. sultanas
3 tablespoons golden syrup

½ teaspoon ground mixed spice
1 large strip lemon peel
3 oz. butter
1 egg
6 tablespoons plain flour
2 teaspoons baking powder
pinch of salt
½ pint milk

Cut the rhubarb into pieces and put into an ovenware dish with the sultanas. Add 1 tablespoon syrup with 4 tablespoons hot water, mixed spice and lemon peel, and pour over the rhubarb. Cream the butter, egg and remaining syrup. Sieve the flour, baking powder and salt. Add to the butter mixture alternately with the milk. Spread over the fruit to cover it completely and bake at 350°F (Gas Mark 5) for 50 minutes.

180°C FAN 160°C

HOT STRAWBERRY COMPOTE

2 lb. strawberries
1 lb. sugar
pinch of ground cinnamon
½ pint red wine
1 dessertspoon honey
1 dessertspoon lemon juice

Clean and hull the strawberries and put into an ovenware dish with the sugar and cinnamon. Cover and bake at 300°F (Gas Mark 2) for 45 minutes. Stir in the wine and continue cooking for 15 minutes. Just before serving, stir in the honey and lemon juice. Serve hot with thick cream.

HOT FRUIT SALAD

1 large grapefruit
2 bananas
juice of ½ lemon
1 oz. soft brown sugar
2 oz. sultanas
2 tablespoons rum

Peel the grapefruit, cut between the sections to remove flesh, but not the skin around sections. Put into a lightly buttered ovenware dish. Cut the bananas into halves across and then downwards to make four pieces. Roll in lemon juice. Put bananas into dish, sprinkle with sugar and sultanas, and add the rum. Cover and bake at 375°F (Gas Mark 5) for 15 minutes. Serve hot with cream.

### BROWN BETTY

1 lb. fresh fruit
6 oz. breadcrumbs
2 oz. melted butter
4 oz. brown sugar
½ lemon
1 teaspoon ground cinnamon

This dish can be made with apples, apricots, peaches, plums or rhubarb. Clean and slice the fruit. Mix the crumbs and butter with a fork and arrange in alternate layers with sliced fruit in a buttered baking dish. On each fruit layer, sprinkle sugar, grated lemon rind and juice, and cinnamon. Finish with a layer of crumbs and pour on ¼ pint hot water. Bake at 350°F (Gas Mark 4) for 40 minutes.

### FRIED FRUIT PIES

8 oz. flaky pastry
16-oz. can fruit salad
1 tablespoon cornflour
deep fat for frying

Roll out pastry ⅛ in. thick, and cut in 4 in. rounds. Drain fruit, and heat syrup to boiling point in a small saucepan. Blend cornflour with a little water, then stir on hot syrup. Cook until just thick, then blend into the drained fruit. Leave until cold. Put a large spoonful of fruit on one half of each pastry round. Damp edges and fold over circles of pastry, pinching edges together to make turnovers. Fry in hot deep fat until crisp and golden and serve hot. These are delicious if served with hot apricot jam as a sauce.

### FRUIT SALAD RING

4 oz. self-raising flour
pinch of salt
½ teaspoon baking powder
4 oz. fresh white breadcrumbs
4 oz. shredded suet
4 oz. caster sugar
grated rind and juice of 1 orange
2 eggs
8-oz. can fruit salad
1½ teaspoons arrowroot

Sift flour, salt and baking powder, and stir in breadcrumbs and suet. Add sugar, orange rind and juice, and beaten eggs, mixing to a soft dropping consistency. Grease a 2-pint ring mould, put in mixture, cover with buttered foil, and steam for 2½ hours. Drain fruit salad, and chop fruit in small pieces. Thicken syrup with arrowroot, and heat chopped fruit in sauce.

### WEARY WILLIE FRUIT MUSH

8 oz. sifted flour
2 teaspoons baking powder
1 teaspoon salt
⅓ pint milk
1 heaped tablespoon butter or margarine
2 lb. blueberries or blackberries
1 lb. sugar
1 teaspoon lemon juice

Sift together flour, baking powder, and salt. Mix with milk and butter. Mix berries, sugar and lemon juice. Combine fruit with batter in a greased covered bowl, and steam for 1 hour. Serve with cream.

Instead of berries, you can use sliced ripe peaches, stoned cherries or stoned plums. The last two will need more sugar so sweeten to taste.

### FRUIT ROLL-UP

6 oz. self-raising flour
pinch of salt
1 teaspoon mixed spice
2 oz. fresh white breadcrumbs
5 oz. shredded suet
1 tablespoon lemon juice
1 tablespoon clear honey
6 oz. mixed dried fruit

Sift flour, salt and spice, add breadcrumbs and suet and mix with lemon juice and a little water to make a soft dough. Roll out to an oblong about 8 in. wide. Spread with honey, and scatter with dried fruit. Roll up carefully and wrap loosely in buttered foil. Steam for 3 hours. Serve with melted honey sharpened with a squeeze of lemon juice.

# (6)

# Cold Puddings

When fruit first comes into season, particularly the summer berries and currants, it is most delicious served simply with sugar and cream. Even the first apples or rhubarb are a pleasure if lightly cooked in the oven with the minimum of liquid, sweetened and chilled and served with cream. But there are many other ways of serving fruit cold which are delicious. Raspberries and strawberries can be sieved and sweetened and used as a sauce for each other, or for raspberries and currants, or over vanilla ice cream. A little liqueur, spirit or wine enhances the fresh fruit flavours. Soft fruits make good fillings for shortcakes, sponges and babas, with plenty of softly whipped cream, and such fillings make the best of small quantities of fruit.

Fools and flummeries are particularly popular, made from fresh or lightly cooked fruit. The simplest fool is a mixture of fruit and cream—today it is usual to sieve the fruit, but traditionally it was only lightly crushed before mixing with the cream. If cream is not obtainable, rich milk or an egg custard may be used instead, but the fruit flavour becomes blurred. Flummeries are thicker mixtures, once consisting of either milk or water thickened with a cereal such as barley or semolina, and not even containing fruit, but today providing an inexpensive fruit dish which may be unmoulded for serving. All cold fruit puddings are better for being served well chilled rather than lukewarm.

### APPLE FLUMMERY

OK but not very exciting
Needs good flavoured apples.

4 tablespoons pearl barley
1½ lb. eating apples
1½ oz. caster sugar
juice of 1 lemon
3 tablespoons double cream

Put the pearl barley into a pan with 2 pints water and bring to the boil. When boiling, add the peeled and sliced apples and simmer until the apples and barley are soft. Put through a sieve and return the purée to the pan with the sugar and lemon juice. Bring to the boil, cool and stir in the cream. Serve chilled.

### APPLE FOAM

2 lb. apples
sugar
2 egg whites
2 × 5 oz. natural yogurt

If possible, use apples which become fluffy when cooked. Peel and core the apples and cook gently without water, but with sugar to taste. When the fruit is tender, sieve or put into a blender, and then cool. Whip the egg whites to stiff peaks and fold into the apple purée with the yogurt. Chill well. This is very good if sprinkled with some thin slices of preserved ginger, or with grated plain chocolate.

### APRICOT COMPOTE

12 oz. dried apricots
1 tablespoon sugar
¼ pint double cream
1 tablespoon brandy or Kirsch

Soak apricots for 5 or 6 hours till well softened. Cover with hot water and sugar and cook for 25 minutes. Allow to cool, and cover with the cream to which the liqueur has been added.

### ICED APRICOT MERINGUE

16-oz. can apricot halves
1 family-size block vanilla ice cream
2 egg whites
6 tablespoons caster sugar

Drain apricots very thoroughly and put into a deep fireproof dish. Put dish in a baking tin filled with ice-cubes. Put spoonfuls of ice cream over fruit. Whip egg whites very stiffly and fold in caster sugar. Cover ice cream completely with this meringue mixture and bake at 450°F (Gas Mark 8) for 3 minutes. Serve at once.

### APRICOT MOUSSE

½ oz. gelatine
16-oz. can apricot halves
2 egg whites
¼ pint double cream

Put gelatine into a small cup with 2 tablespoons of water and leave for 5 minutes, then put cup into a pan of very hot water, so the gelatine becomes thin and clear. Drain the apricot halves and put the fruit and *half* the syrup through a sieve. Whip egg whites until stiff peaks form, and whip cream until just stiff. Add the purée to the cream and fold in the gelatine. Lightly fold in the egg whites and put into a bowl. Serve chilled.

### APRICOT GÂTEAU

3 eggs
4½ oz. caster sugar
3 oz. plain flour
16-oz. can apricot halves
4 oz. apricot jam

Whisk eggs and sugar together in a bowl over hot water until very thick and almost white. Remove from heat and continue whisking for 3 minutes, then fold in the sifted flour. Put into an 8 in. sponge tin and bake at 375°F (Gas Mark 5) for 40 minutes. Cool on a wire rack. Split the cake and sandwich together with a thin layer of apricot jam. Drain the apricots very thoroughly. Warm remaining jam and spread a little on top of the cake. Cover with apricot halves and brush with remaining jam. Leave to set. If liked, whipped cream may be put in the centre of the cake, and used for decoration.

### BLACKBERRY AND APPLE COMPOTE

1 lb. blackberries
2 large eating apples
8 oz. sugar
4 tablespoons water

Wash the blackberries and put them into a pan with the

peeled and sliced apples, sugar and water. Bring to the boil, cover and simmer for about 5 minutes until the apple slices are tender but not broken. Chill before serving with cream.

### BLACKBERRY FLUMMERY

1 lb. blackberries
8 oz. sugar
2 tablespoons cornflour
pinch of salt
1 teaspoon lemon juice

Simmer the blackberries and sugar with 6 tablespoons water until soft. Put through a sieve and thicken with the cornflour mixed with a little water, and the salt. Simmer for 5 minutes, stirring well. Add the lemon juice and cool. Serve chilled with cream.

### BLACKBERRY PUDDING

1 lb. blackberries
½ pint cider
8 oz. caster sugar
5 large slices white bread

Simmer the blackberries with the cider and sugar until soft. Remove the crusts from the bread and use some of the bread to line a pudding basin. Pour the hot fruit into the basin and cover with the remaining bread. Put a plate and a weight on top and leave in a cold place for 24 hours. Turn out and serve with cream. If liked, some apples may be cooked with the blackberries, and additional layers of bread can be put into the pudding to make it more firm and filling.

### SPICED CHERRIES

1 lb. red eating cherries
4 oz. caster sugar
½ teaspoon ground cinnamon
½ teaspoon ground nutmeg
pinch of ground cloves
4 oz. redcurrant jelly

Stone the cherries and put the fruit into a covered pan with

4 tablespoons water, sugar and spices. Simmer for 10 minutes and then lift out the cherries and put them into a serving bowl. Add the redcurrant jelly to the cooking liquid and boil down until syrupy. Pour over the cherries and chill. Serve with whipped cream.

This mixture is also very good served hot as a sauce over vanilla ice cream.

### CHERRY TART

8 oz. shortcrust pastry
8 oz. stoned cooking cherries
4 oz. ground almonds
6 oz. icing sugar
2 eggs
¼ pint double cream

Line a flan tin and prick the pastry well. Fill with cherries. Mix ground almonds, sugar and eggs, one at a time, to a soft paste. Pour over the cherries and bake at 425°F (Gas Mark 7) for 30 minutes. Serve cold with whipped cream.

### GOOSEBERRY FLUMMERY

1 lb. gooseberries
8 oz. sugar
1 teaspoon lemon juice
½ pint milk
4 level tablespoons fine semolina
green vegetable colouring

Simmer the gooseberries with the sugar and 4 tablespoons water in a covered saucepan, until the skins burst and the fruit is pulpy. Take off the heat and add the lemon juice. Warm the milk and sprinkle in the semolina. Bring to the boil and simmer for 3 minutes to thicken. Take off the heat and stir in the gooseberries. Colour green very lightly if liked, and pour into a bowl to set.

Rhubarb may be used instead of gooseberries if liked (tinted pink instead of green), and the fruit may be sieved for those who like a smooth texture.

GOOSEBERRY FOOL

1 lb. gooseberries
8 oz. sugar
¾ pint double cream

Simmer the gooseberries with sugar and ¼ pint water until the fruit is soft. Put through a sieve and mix with the cream. A dessertspoon of orange-flower water adds a delicate flavour.

LEMON FLUMMERY

¾ oz. butter
1 lemon
1 oz. plain flour
4 oz. caster sugar
1 egg
2 oz. biscuit or macaroon crumbs

Boil the butter with ½ pint water and the grated lemon peel. Mix the flour and sugar in a bowl and make a well in the centre. Pour in the hot liquid, whisking to avoid lumps. Mix the egg yolk with a little of the hot flour mixture, and then return all the liquid to the pan. Bring slowly to the boil and cook gently for 10 minutes. Remove from the heat and add the juice of the lemon. Pour into a bowl and fold in the stiffly whisked egg white. Cool and then scatter the crumbs over the surface. Serve very cold with cream.

LEMON SOLID

1 oz. gelatine
1½ pints milk
½ pint single cream
5 oz. granulated sugar
2 lemons

Put the gelatine to stand in 1 pint of milk. Put the remaining milk and cream into a pan with the sugar. Warm gently until the sugar has melted and just bring it to the boil. Add the grated rind of the lemons. Pour in the milk and gelatine mixture and slowly stir in the lemon juice. The mixture will look slightly curdled. Pour into a mould, set in a cold place, and turn out.

LEMON TARTS

*Pastry:*
4 oz. butter
2 oz. icing sugar
juice of 1 lemon
6 oz. plain flour
½ teaspoon salt

*Filling:*
1 egg
5 oz. sugar
1 lemon
2 oz. softened butter

Cream butter and icing sugar, add lemon juice and flour sifted with salt. Mix to a firm paste using very little water. Chill 15 minutes. Put into tart cases, prick and bake blind at 450°F (Gas Mark 8) for 10 minutes.

To make the filling, beat egg with sugar until light and creamy. Add juice and grated rind of lemon, and softened butter and continue beating to a smooth paste. Fill tarts with mixture and bake at 325°F (Gas Mark 3) for 10-15 minutes, or till filling is firm. Cool before serving.

CARAMELISED ORANGES

10 oz. caster sugar
2 tablespoons butter
6 sweet juicy oranges
toasted flaked almonds

Put the sugar in a strong pan and stir constantly over low heat until it turns to a light golden colour, then remove from heat and add butter, stirring until smooth. Peel the oranges carefully, removing as much pith as possible, slice thinly and put on a serving dish in overlapping layers. Pour over the caramel sauce and scatter with flaked almonds. Whipped cream may be served.

AMBROSIA

8 juicy oranges
4 oz. caster sugar
4 oz. desiccated coconut

Peel the oranges and remove all the white pith. Slice the oranges thinly crosswise and put into a dish in alternate layers with the sugar and coconut. Chill thoroughly before serving. A mixture of oranges and pineapple is very good.

For a special occasion, sprinkle the oranges with a little gin or light rum.

### FROZEN PEACHES

8 large ripe peaches
1 lb. sugar
¼ pint brandy or whisky
2 tablespoons dark rum

Peel and stone the peaches and cut them into very thin slices. Cover them with the sugar and leave to stand for an hour, turning once or twice. Add the brandy or whisky and rum and pack 1 in. deep in one or two freezing trays. Turn the refrigerator setting to the lowest point and put the freezing trays into the ice-making compartment. Freeze for 90 minutes, stirring two or three times. When the peaches begin to get hard, they are ready to serve in small portions with thick cream.

### PEACH BABA

4½ oz. plain flour
pinch of salt
½ oz. sugar
½ oz. fresh yeast (or ¼ oz. dried yeast)
4 fl. oz. warm milk
2 eggs
1¾ oz. butter
16-oz. can peach slices

Sift flour and salt into a bowl. Cream sugar and yeast and pour in milk. Blend well together, then add flour, together with beaten eggs, and beat well with a wooden spoon for 5 minutes. Cover the bowl and leave in a warm place for 45 minutes, until double in bulk. Cream butter until soft and beat into the dough for 5 minutes. Pour into a buttered ring tin and leave in warm place for 10 minutes. Bake at 450°F (Gas Mark 8) for 30 minutes until deep golden brown. If no ring tin is available, put a cocoa tin in the centre of an 8 in. cake tin and hold it firmly in place while pouring in the batter.

Drain the peaches, reserving the syrup. When cake is

cooked, turn on to a wire rack and baste thoroughly while still hot with the syrup. Catch the syrup under the rack with a soup plate, and continue pouring over the cake until it is thoroughly soaked and glistening. Remove to serving plate, and fill centre with peaches. Serve with whipped cream.

### PEACH SHORTCAKE

8 oz. plain flour
2 teaspoons baking powder
½ teaspoon salt
1 tablespoon sugar
2 oz. butter
¼ pint milk
pinch of nutmeg
butter
16-oz. can peach slices
whipped cream

Sift flour, baking powder and salt, and stir in sugar. Work in butter and mix to a dough with milk. Add a little nutmeg if liked. Divide pastry into two pieces and lightly roll out to fit buttered sandwich tin. Put one piece in the tin, spread lightly with melted butter and put other half on top. Bake at 450°F (Gas Mark 8) for 12 minutes. Split the layers carefully and spread with butter, then put halves together again with drained peach slices between. Cover top with whipped cream and garnish with remaining peach slices. Serve while very fresh.

### PEAR MERINGUE

4 egg whites
1 teaspoon vinegar
1 level teaspoon cornflour
10 oz. caster sugar
½ pint double cream
2 oz. plain chocolate
16-oz. can pear halves

Set oven at 250°F (Gas Mark 1) and put a piece of buttered paper on a flat oven tray. Beat egg whites to soft peaks, then gradually add vinegar and cornflour, and all the sugar, beating well all the time. Continue beating until the mixture stands in stiff peaks. Spread on to buttered paper in a circle about 8 in. diameter, and bake for 1¼ hours. Lift on to a flat serving dish. Whip cream stiffly and fold in grated chocolate, leaving a little for decoration. Pile cream on to the meringue case, arrange drained pear halves on top, and sprinkle with remaining chocolate.

### PEARS IN HONEY SYRUP

8 oz. seeded raisins
4 large pears
4 oz. honey
½ teaspoon cinnamon

Soak raisins in warm water for 1 hour and drain well. Peel pears, leaving them whole. Boil honey with ½ pint water, add pears and cinnamon, and poach until just tender when tested with a fork. Drain pears, saving syrup, and arrange in centre of serving bowl. Put raisins into syrup and simmer for 5 minutes. Remove from heat, cool slightly, and arrange raisins round pears. Pour over syrup. Chill and serve very cold with small sweet biscuits and thin cream.

### ROYAL PEARS

2 oz. pudding rice
¾ pint milk
10 oz. sugar
1 teaspoon vanilla essence
2 egg yolks
¼ pint double cream
4 large pears
juice of 1 lemon

Boil rice in water for 2 minutes and drain. Bring milk to the boil, add drained rice, reduce heat and cook uncovered over a very low heat for 15 minutes until rice is tender. Remove from heat and stir in 2 oz. sugar and vanilla essence. Stir in beaten egg yolks and cool thoroughly. When rice is cold, stir in whipped cream carefully so rice grains are not crushed, and put into serving bowl. Boil remaining 8 oz. sugar with ½ pint water, reduce heat and simmer whole or halved peeled pears until just tender. Drain well, reserving syrup. Arrange pears on rice. Add lemon juice to syrup, cool and pour over pears.

### SPICED RAISIN FLAN

8 oz. digestive biscuits
4 oz. butter
8 oz. seeded raisins
⅓ pint water
1 tablespoon cornflour
¼ teaspoon ground cloves
¼ teaspoon ground cinnamon
4 oz. soft brown sugar

Crush biscuits into coarse crumbs with a rolling pin, and stir into melted butter. Press into a greased 7 in. sponge tin or pie plate to form a flan case, and chill in the refrigerator. Simmer raisins gently in water for 10 minutes, then blend in cornflour which has been stirred into a tablespoon of cold water. Stir gently until thickened, and add spices and sugar. Continue heating and stirring until sugar has just melted. Cool and put into flan case. Serve cold with cream.

### RASPBERRIES IN REDCURRANT SAUCE

1 lb. raspberries
8 oz. redcurrants
6 oz. sugar

Put the raspberries into a serving bowl. Simmer the redcurrants with the sugar and 6 tablespoons water. Cook for 15 minutes, and put through a sieve. Chill the redcurrant sauce and pour over the raspberries.

### CREAM CROWDIE

2 oz. coarse oatmeal
1 pint double cream
2 oz. caster sugar
1 tablespoon rum
4 oz. ripe raspberries or blackberries

Put the oatmeal in a thick-bottomed saucepan and shake over

heat until the oatmeal is crisp. Whip the cream to soft peaks and stir in the oatmeal, sugar, rum and fruit. Serve at once.

### RHUBARB SUMMER CHARLOTTE

1 lb. young rhubarb
4 oz. sugar
2 oz. butter
6 oz. fresh white breadcrumbs
2 oz. soft brown sugar
¼ pint double cream

Cut the rhubarb into 1 in. lengths and cook in 2 tablespoons water and the sugar until the fruit is tender, and then cool. Melt the butter, take off the heat, and stir in the breadcrumbs and brown sugar. Put a layer of the crumb mixture into a serving bowl. Add a layer of rhubarb, and continue with layers of crumbs and rhubarb. Top with a layer of softly whipped cream.

For additional flavour, add a little grated lemon or orange rind to the rhubarb, or a pinch of ginger. For a stronger colour and flavour, cook the rhubarb in 4 oz. raspberry jam instead of water and sugar.

### STRAWBERRIES IN ORANGE LIQUEUR

1½ lb. ripe strawberries
4 oz. caster sugar
3 tablespoons orange juice – squash OK
1 tablespoon Grand Marnier or Curaçao
sweetened whipped cream

Hull the strawberries and toss them in the sugar. Sprinkle with the orange juice and liqueur. Stand the bowl in a larger bowl filled with ice cubes and serve with sweetened whipped cream.

### STRAWBERRY AND RASPBERRY FOOL

8 oz. strawberries
8 oz. raspberries
4 oz. caster sugar
¾ pint double cream

Crush the strawberries and raspberries and put them through

a sieve. Mix the purée with the sugar and cream. Serve well chilled, if possible decorated with a few whole fruit.

### STRAWBERRY CREAM

bit runny - added cornflour

1 lb. strawberries
1 miniature bottle Kirsch or 3 tablespoonfuls
½ pint milk
2 eggs
5 tablespoons caster sugar
½ pint cream
3 drops rosewater

This is a very good way of turning a small quantity of fruit into a large, rich pudding for a party. If the strawberries are large, cut them in half, but leave small ones whole. Put them into a bowl with half the Kirsch. Make a custard with the milk, egg yolks, and 1 tablespoon sugar. Chill and mix in remaining Kirsch. Whip the cream and rosewater. Fold the custard into the cream and then fold in stiffly whipped egg whites, strawberries and Kirsch, and the remaining sugar. Serve very cold.

### STRAWBERRIES ROMANOFF

1 lb. strawberries
3 tablespoons caster sugar
1 sherry glass dry white wine
½ pint double cream

Wash, hull and slice the strawberries, reserving a few whole for decoration. Put the sliced strawberries in a bowl and sprinkle with caster sugar. Pour over the wine and leave for an hour or so, turning the fruit gently a couple of times. Whip the cream until thick. Stir in the strawberry juices and fold in the sliced strawberries. Turn into serving dishes and decorate with the whole strawberries.

### SUMMER FRUIT BOWL

1 lb. gooseberries
4 oz. redcurrants
4 oz. blackcurrants
4 oz. raspberries
6 oz. caster sugar

Top and tail the gooseberries and remove the stalks from the redcurrants and blackcurrants. Put into a saucepan with the sugar and ¼ pint water. Bring slowly to the boil and simmer for 5 minutes without breaking the fruit. Cool and stir in the raspberries. Serve very cold with cream. If liked, add a little Kirsch to the cold fruit before serving.

### FRUIT CREAM

2 large tablespoons apricot jam
3 eggs
1 tablespoon sugar
¾ pint hot milk
8-oz. can fruit cocktail
3 tablespoons whipped cream
1 oz. grated chocolate

Spread the apricot jam in the base of a soufflé dish. Put two of the eggs and one egg yolk into a bowl, mix with the sugar, and pour on the hot milk. Blend well and strain into the soufflé dish. Put the dish into a tin half full of hot water, cover with a piece of paper, and cook at 325°F (Gas Mark 3) for 45 minutes. Leave until cold. Drain the fruit cocktail and spread fruit lightly on surface. Whip remaining egg white stiffly, fold into whipped cream, and cover the fruit. Sprinkle with grated chocolate and serve cold.

### PAVLOVA

4 egg whites
10 oz. caster sugar
1 teaspoon vinegar
1 level teaspoon cornflour
½ pint double cream
canned or fresh fruits

Set oven at 250°F (Gas Mark 1). Place a piece of buttered paper on a flat oven tray. Beat egg whites for 1 minute. Gradually add sugar, beating well all the time. Add vinegar and cornflour. Continue beating until the mixture is stiff enough to stand alone in peaks. Tip on to buttered paper in a perfect round about 8 in. diameter and pile up in centre. Bake for 1-1¼ hours. Lift on to a flat serving dish. Cover with whipped cream, whole or sliced canned or fresh fruit. If liked, stir 2 teaspoonfuls of rum or any suitable liqueur into the cream after whipping.

# (7)

# Ices and Sorbets

Fresh fruit ice creams and sorbets are not difficult to make and provide a delicious and refreshing ending to a meal. If a sorbetière is available, the ice can be put into this to freeze, and the 'paddles' will beat the ice as it freezes so that it remains smooth.

Without this small machine, it is usually necessary to beat the ice once or twice during freezing so that it does not set hard or contain ice crystals. The partly frozen ice should be taken from the freezing tray and put into a chilled bowl. It can then be beaten by hand or electric mixer—an electric blender can also be used for beating if preferred. Ices are best frozen in the ice-making compartment of a refrigerator which provides the correct temperature when turned to lowest setting. After the final beating the ice should be covered with a piece of foil to prevent crystals forming. When the ice has been frozen, the refrigerator setting can be returned to normal so that the ice can ripen before serving. If ices are being made for freezer storage, it is best to make them this way, and then repack them into suitable containers for freezer storage.

A very simple ice may be made by freezing fruit purée (made from fresh or cooked fruit), sweetened lightly to taste. This is in fact the best way of freezing strawberries to retain the fresh fruit flavour and colour. A little orange or lemon juice may be added to the fruit or a few drops of brandy, Kirsch or other liqueur.

A simple cream ice can be made by mixing sweetened fruit purée with an equal quantity of whipped cream (this is particularly good made with fresh strawberries or raspberries, or with fresh apricots lightly poached in a sugar syrup.)

### APPLE ICE CREAM

½ pint apple purée
pinch of ground nutmeg
pinch of ground cinnamon

2 teaspoons lemon juice
sugar
½ pint cream

Mix apple purée and spices and lemon juice and sweeten very lightly to taste. Chill for 1 hour. Fold in whipped cream and pour into freezing tray. Freeze until firm. This ice is very good with butterscotch or raspberry sauce.

### APPLE SORBET WITH SULTANA SAUCE

1½ lb. cooking apples
6 oz. caster sugar
2 lemons
1 in. cinnamon stick
1 pint water
green vegetable colouring
2 fl. oz. brandy
¼ pint double cream

*Sultana Sauce:*
8 oz. sultanas
½ pint water
1 oz. rum
3 oz. caster sugar
1 bay leaf
strip of lemon peel

Peel and slice the apples and put them into a pan with the sugar, peel of 1 lemon, cinnamon and water. Cook until the apples are soft. Add the juice of 2 lemons and colour lightly green. Put through a sieve, cool and add the brandy. Freeze to a thick batter, add whipped cream and continue freezing for 1½ hours.

Make the sauce by simmering all the ingredients together until they are of the consistency of thick cream. Take out the bay leaf and lemon peel, and chill before serving over the apple sorbet.

### BLACKBERRY ICE

4 oz. caster sugar
¼ pint water
2 rose geranium leaves
*or* 1 tablespoon rosewater
1 lb. blackberries

Boil together the sugar and water for 5 minutes and leave to cool with the rose geranium leaves or rosewater stirred in. Wash the blackberries and press them through a sieve. Mix the fruit and syrup. Pour into a refrigerator freezing tray, cover with foil and freeze at normal ice-making temperature for 2 hours.

BLACKCURRANT SORBET

1 lb. blackcurrants
2 oz. icing sugar
2 × 5-oz. natural yogurt
juice of ½ lemon
½ oz. gelatine
4 tablespoons water
2 egg whites

Put the blackcurrants into a pan with ½ pint water and simmer until the fruit is soft. Put through a sieve. Mix this blackcurrant purée with the icing sugar, yogurt and lemon juice in a bowl. Dissolve the gelatine in the water over a pan of hot water until it becomes syrupy. Stir this into the purée. When the mixture begins to set, fold in the stiffly whipped egg whites. Pour into an ice tray and freeze.

BLUEBERRY FREEZE

1 lb. blueberries
4 oz. caster sugar
pinch of salt
½ pint double cream

Crush the blueberries and stir in the sugar and salt. Fold in the lightly whipped cream. Freeze for 45 minutes. Serve with a grating of lemon rind on each portion.

CRANBERRY ICE

8 oz. cranberries
1 teaspoon gelatine
2 tablespoons lemon juice
½ pint orange juice
12 oz. sugar
2 egg whites

Wash the cranberries and cook them in ¾ pint water with a lid on for 10 minutes. Put through a sieve. Soften the gelatine in 2 tablespoons cold water and stand the bowl in hot water until the gelatine is syrupy. Stir the gelatine into lemon and orange juices, sugar and cranberry pulp, and stir well until the sugar has dissolved. Freeze in a refrigerator tray for about 1 hour until mushy. Beat well and fold in the egg whites whipped to soft peaks. Freeze for about 2 hours until firm, then break up the mixture again and beat until smooth and firm. Return to freezing tray for 30 minutes.

GOOSEBERRY ICE

1 lb. gooseberries
4 oz. caster sugar
½ pint double cream

Wash the gooseberries and put in a pan without topping and tailing. Add 1 teaspoon water and sugar and simmer with a lid on for 15 minutes until fruit is soft. Put through a sieve and cool the purée. Whip cream into peaks and fold into the purée, adding a little green colouring if liked. Put into ice tray and freeze for 2 hours. Whisk in a cold basin until smooth and creamy, return to freezer and freeze for 1 hour.

GOOSEBERRY SORBET

2 lb. gooseberries
6 oz. caster sugar
1½ pints water
juice of 1 lemon
green vegetable colouring
2 fl. oz. Maraschino
2 fl. oz. rum

Cook gooseberries with sugar and water, add lemon juice and a little green colouring and put through a sieve. Cool and freeze to a thick batter. Add Maraschino and rum, and continue freezing. This ice will not become solid.

LEMON CREAM ICE

2 lemons
3 oz. sugar
¼ pint water
¼ pint double cream

Peel the lemons thinly and put the peel with the sugar and water. Simmer gently for 5 minutes and leave until cool. Take out the peel. Add the lemon juice to the syrup and leave until completely cold. Whip the cream softly and gradually pour on the lemon syrup. Put into an ice tray and freeze for two hours, stirring twice during freezing.

### LEMON SHERBET

4 lemons
4 egg whites
1 teaspoon grated lemon rind
sugar

Halve the lemons and scoop out the pulp. Squeeze out the juice from the pulp. Whip the egg whites stiffly and add the lemon juice, grated rind and a little sugar to taste. Freeze in an ice tray, stirring frequently. Serve the ice in the lemon half shells.

### FROZEN ORANGE PUDDING

3 eggs
juice of 1 orange
juice of 1 lemon
4 oz. sugar
pinch of salt
½ pint double cream
12 macaroons

Beat egg yolks and add orange and lemon juice, sugar and salt and cook in a bowl over boiling water until thick. Cool and add stiffly beaten egg whites and softly whipped cream. Crush the macaroons into crumbs with a rolling pin. Put half the crumbs in an ice-making tray, top with the orange mixture, and then with remaining macaroon crumbs. Freeze in the ice-making compartment of a refrigerator for 4 hours.

### ORANGE SORBET

2 teaspoons gelatine
½ pint water
6 oz. sugar
1 teaspoon grated lemon rind

1 teaspoon grated orange rind
½ pint orange juice
4 tablespoons lemon juice
2 egg whites

Soak gelatine in a little of the water and boil the rest of the water and sugar for 10 minutes to a syrup. Stir gelatine into syrup and cool. Add rinds and juices. Beat egg whites until stiff but not dry and fold into mixture. Freeze to a mush, beat once, then continue freezing allowing 3 hours total freezing time. (This ice will not go completely hard.)

*Lemon Sorbet*: Follow the same method, using only lemon juice and rind to make up the total quantities, instead of a mixture of orange and lemon.

*Fresh Fruit Cases*: Orange and lemon sorbets are particularly attractive if packed into fruit skins. Scoop out the oranges or lemons, wash thoroughly and dry and pack in sorbet when it is ready for storage, leaving surface raised above fruit skins. Wrap containers in foil for storage. If this is not done before storage, the skins may be prepared and left wet and the sorbet packed in and returned unwrapped to the freezer for 1 hour before serving.

### RASPBERRY CREAM ICE

8 oz. raspberries
3 tablespoons icing sugar
½ pint double cream

Sieve the raspberries and stir in the sugar. Whip the cream softly and fold in the raspberry purée. Freeze without stirring.

### RASPBERRY HONEY ICE

1 lb. raspberries
¼ pint double cream
5 oz. natural yogurt
10 level tablespoons honey
2 tablespoons lemon juice
pinch of salt
4 egg whites

Sieve the raspberries and mix the purée with the cream, yogurt, honey, lemon juice and salt. Put into an ice tray and freeze to a thick batter. Put into a chilled bowl, beat well and fold in the stiffly whisked egg whites. Return the mixture to the ice tray and freeze.

REDCURRANT ICE

1 lb. redcurrants
4 oz. redcurrant jelly
1 pint water
1 large ripe tomato
4 oz. raspberries
juice and rind of ½ lemon
3 oz. caster sugar
red vegetable colouring
4 egg yolks
2 fl. oz. brandy
½ pint double cream

Remove currants from stalks and simmer with redcurrant jelly, hot water, tomato, raspberries, juice and rind of lemon, sugar and colouring until the fruit is a pulp. Cool and add well-beaten egg yolks and brandy. Rub through a sieve, and freeze to a batter. Add whipped cream and continue freezing for 2 hours.

STRAWBERRY WATER ICE

12 oz. sugar
¾ pint water
8 oz. strawberries
juice of 1 orange
1 egg white

Dissolve the sugar in water for 5 minutes. Cool and add crushed strawberries and orange juice. Freeze in a refrigerator tray. When half frozen, put into a chilled bowl, crush and add the stiffly whipped egg white. Beat well and return to the refrigerator until frozen.

# (8)

# Hot and Cold Drinks

Drinks made with fresh fruit can be refreshing and cooling in the summer, or warming and soothing in winter. It was traditional to make fruit syrups ready for winter use which were diluted with hot water or mixed with spirits to warm chilled travellers and stave off colds—probably a forerunner of today's Vitamin C drinks for children. Obviously summer soft fruits are easiest to use because they can be so easily sieved or heated to extract juice, but apples are also a useful basis for drinks. Orange and lemon juices are easily available, while bananas are excellent in milk drinks to make nourishing meals-in-a-glass.

### APPLE SHERBET

2 large cooking apples
½ teaspoon ground ginger
1 tablespoon sugar
soda water

Do not peel, but cut the apples into very thin slices. Put into an ovenware casserole with ginger and sugar, and ½ pint boiling water. Bake at 300°F (Gas Mark 2) for 1½ hours. Cool and strain off liquid, and serve chilled with soda water.

### APPLE TISANE

2 large sour apples
6 raisins
1 tablespoon sugar

Bake the apples until soft and cut them into quarters. Add the raisins and sugar, and pour over ½ pint boiling water. Cover and leave in a warm place by the side of a fire or on the stove for 1 hour. Strain off liquid to drink.

### BANANA FLIP

4 bananas
8 oz. cottage cheese
1 pint milk
2 tablespoons brown sugar

Mash the bananas and beat in sieved cottage cheese. They may be mixed together in a blender if preferred. Gradually whisk in the milk and sweeten with the brown sugar. Serve very cold.

### HOT BLACKCURRANT PUNCH

1 lb. blackcurrants
1 lemon
6 tablespoons sherry
½ pint claret
sugar

Simmer the blackcurrants in 1 pint water until soft. Put through a sieve. Add the thinly pared rind of the lemon and the juice, the sherry and claret. Heat slowly and add sugar to taste. Gradually add an additional ½ pint hot water. Remove the rind and serve hot in mugs. A sprinkling of grated cinnamon, or a slice of lemon can be used for each serving. This is a good cold weather drink, and can be made from frozen blackcurrants.

### CHERRY BRANDY

1 lb. Morello cherries
4 oz. candy sugar
½ in. cinnamon stick
brandy

Remove stalks from the cherries, wipe the fruit and prick it with a thick needle. Half-fill wide-necked preserving jars with the cherries. Add the sugar and cinnamon, and fill the jars to the top with brandy. Cover tightly and leave for 6 months. Drain off the brandy for drinking, and use the cherries to eat as a pudding with cream. Candy sugar can usually be obtained from suppliers of wine-making accessories. If it is not available, use granulated sugar.

### CRANBERRY COCKTAIL

1 lb. cranberries
4 oz. sugar
2 tablespoons orange juice

Cook the cranberries in 1 pint water until the skins burst. Squeeze through muslin to extract all the liquid and add the sugar. Stir over low heat until dissolved. Chill and stir in the orange juice. Serve with ice cubes.

### SPICED ELDERBERRY SYRUP

elderberries
sugar
cloves
root ginger

Stalk the elderberries, put them into a casserole with a lid and cook in the oven at 300°F (Gas Mark 2). When the juice runs, pour it off into a pan. Return the jar to the oven and continue cooking and straining off juice until no more juice runs. To every pint of juice, add 8 oz. sugar, 6 cloves and a small piece of ginger. Put into a pan and bring to the boil. Simmer for 30 minutes, strain into bottles and cork tightly. Dilute with hot water as a winter drink to soothe a cold. Bottled syrups can sometimes blow off corks which are not tied down, but syrups can be frozen instead.

### FRESH LEMONADE

4 large lemons
2 lb. sugar
1 dessertspoon tartaric acid

Squeeze the lemons over sugar in a basin. Add the tartaric acid and pour on 2 pints boiling water. Stir well to dissolve sugar. Cool and bottle. Dilute with water or soda water to taste.

### ORANGE PUNCH

2 tablespoons tea leaves (Indian is best)
¼ pint orange juice
4 tablespoons lemon juice
sugar
1 pint ginger ale
whisky (optional)

Boil 1¼ pints water and pour on to the tea leaves. Leave to

brew for 5 minutes. Stir well and strain on to the orange and lemon juices. Sweeten lightly to taste. Chill well and just before serving add the ginger ale and some ice cubes. For a party, decorate with some orange slices and mint sprigs. For an alcoholic punch, add whisky to taste.

### ORANGE AND GRAPEFRUIT SQUASH

2 lb. sugar
2 large oranges
1 grapefruit
4 level teaspoons tartaric acid

Put the sugar into a bowl and add the finely grated rind and the juice of the oranges and grapefruit. Add 1½ pints boiling water and the tartaric acid. Stir until the sugar has dissolved and leave to cool. When completely cold, put into bottles. Dilute with water to taste for a refreshing drink.

### ORANGE AND LIME FIZZ

½ pint orange juice
2 oz. sugar
6 mint sprigs
6 tablespoons lime juice
soda water

Put half the orange juice into a pan with the sugar. Strip the mint leaves from their stems and add to the juice and sugar. Bring to the boil and then cool. Add the remaining orange and lime juice. Pour over ice cubes and top up with soda water.

### HONEY ORANGE CRUSH

1 lb. granulated sugar
8 oz. honey
1 oz. citric acid
4 oranges

Put sugar, honey and citric acid in a bowl, together with juice and thinly pared orange rind. Pour on 2 pints boiling water. Stir until sugar dissolves, then leave to cool. Strain, and put into bottles. Use 2 tablespoons of this syrup to a tumbler of hot water. For a party, float a slice of orange in each tumbler.

PEACH GINGER

2 peaches
3 oz. caster sugar
¼ teaspoon ground ginger
nutmeg
2 tablespoons lemon juice
1 pint ginger beer
2 slices orange

Sieve the peaches and mix with the sugar, ginger, a pinch of nutmeg and lemon juice. Put into two long glasses and chill for 30 minutes. Top up with ginger beer and garnish with orange slices.

RASPBERRY SHAKE

8 oz. ripe raspberries
1½ pints milk
1 oz. sugar
pinch of salt
4 scoops of ice cream

Crush the raspberries and mix with the milk. Put through a sieve, pressing out all the liquid. Stir in the sugar and salt. Put a scoop of ice cream into each glass and top up with raspberry milk. Serve at once.

RASPBERRY VINEGAR

2 lb. raspberries
1 pint white vinegar
sugar

Put the berries into a jar and mash them well. Pour on the vinegar and leave covered for six days, stirring the mixture each day. Strain through a jelly bag without pressing. For each pint of liquid, allow 1 lb. sugar, and stir gently together over a low heat until the sugar has dissolved. Boil gently for ten minutes, removing scum. Leave until cold, pour into bottles and cork well. Dilute with warm water for colds, or use as a syrup with plain puddings.

### RHUBARB PUNCH

1½ lb. rhubarb
12 oz. sugar
¼ pint orange juice
4 tablespoons lemon juice
pinch of salt
soda water

Cut the rhubarb into small pieces and simmer in 2 pints water until soft. Put through a sieve, and then squeeze through a piece of muslin to extract all the liquid. Stir in the sugar until dissolved. Bring to the boil, and add the orange and lemon juices and salt. Chill and serve with plenty of ice and soda water.

### SLOE GIN

1 lb. sloes
8 oz. candy sugar
1 teaspoon pure almond essence
gin

If sloes are not available, this may be made with damsons.

Wash the fruit well and prick with a thick needle. Half-fill a preserving jar with the fruit and add the sugar and almond essence. Top up the jar with gin. Screw on the lid and keep in a warm place for a week, shaking the jar at least three times a day. Store in a cool dark place and drain off the liquid into a bottle after three months. Candy sugar can usually be obtained from suppliers of wine-making accessories. If it is not available, use granulated sugar. It is important to use pure almond essence and not a synthetic substitute.

### STRAWBERRY SYRUP

2½ lb. strawberries
1 oz. tartaric acid
sugar

Dissolve the acid in 1 pint cold water and pour on to the strawberries. Leave for 24 hours and strain through muslin. To each pint of liquid, add 1½ lb. sugar and leave until dissolved. Put into bottles and leave uncorked for 5 days in a cool place; then cork tightly. Serve diluted with soda water or plain water, or use as a sauce for ices or puddings.

### CIDER RAISIN PUNCH

4 oz. raisins
½ pint water
12 cloves
1½ pints sweet cider
5 tablespoons rum
2 tablespoons lemon juice
1 orange

Bring the raisins, water and cloves slowly to the boil, and simmer for 5 minutes. Leave until cold. Add the cider, rum, lemon juice and thinly sliced orange, and heat without boiling. Serve hot with a few raisins and orange slice in each glass.

(9)

# Fresh Fruit Cakes

Cakes made with fresh fruit are light and delicious and can be used at teatime, or as a light pudding for lunch or supper. They are also very useful for picnic meals, being easy to carry and combining the sweetness and fruit flavour which is refreshing at the end of an outdoor meal. Apples are particularly useful in cake-making giving a light moist texture to shortcakes, fruitcakes and gingerbreads.

### CIDER APPLE CAKE

¼ pint cider
6 oz. butter
6 oz. light soft brown sugar
3 eggs
6 oz. self-raising flour
1 cooking apple

Put the cider into a small saucepan, bring to the boil and boil steadily until the cider is reduced to 2 tablespoons. Leave to cool. Cream together the butter and sugar until light and fluffy. Gradually beat in the beaten eggs and then fold in the flour. Spread half the mixture over the base of a greased 7 in. cake tin. Peel, core and grate the apple and spread evenly over the surface. Cover with the remaining cake mixture and spread level. Bake at 400°F (Gas Mark 6) for 20 minutes, and then at 325°F (Gas Mark 3) for 5 minutes. Turn out and cool on a rack. Just before serving, dust the top with icing sugar.

### APPLE CHEESECAKES

8 oz. thick apple purée
4 oz. caster sugar
4 oz. melted butter
2 eggs and 2 yolks
1 lemon
12 oz. puff pastry

Add the apple purée to the sugar and butter, eggs and egg yolks. Add the grated lemon rind and juice and mix well. Line some tartlet tins with the pastry, fill with the apple mixture, and bake at 375°F (Gas Mark 5) for 25 minutes.

### APPLE CRACKLE CAKE

8 oz. self-raising flour
pinch of salt
1 teaspoon ground cinnamon
½ teaspoon ground nutmeg
4 oz. butter
4 oz. caster sugar
8 oz. eating apples
2 eggs
6 tablespoons milk

*Topping:*
2 tablespoons caster sugar
½ oz. butter

Sift the flour into a bowl with salt, cinnamon and nutmeg. Rub in the butter and stir in the sugar. Peel the apples and slice them finely. Stir into the dry mixture and mix to a batter with eggs and milk. Turn into a well-greased 7 in. cake tin with a removable bottom. Cover the top with caster sugar and the butter cut into flakes. Bake at 375°F (Gas Mark 5) for 45 minutes, then at 350°F (Gas Mark 4) for 30 minutes. Remove carefully from the tin so that the topping is not disturbed. The cake may be eaten warm with cream, custard or ice cream, or it can be served cold, spread with butter.

### DORSET APPLE CAKE

8 oz. self-raising flour
pinch of salt
4 oz. cooking fat
12 oz. eating apples
4 oz. sugar
2 oz. currants
milk
3 oz. butter
1 tablespoon brown sugar

Sift the flour and salt and rub in the cooking fat until the mixture is like breadcrumbs. Peel and core the apples and chop them roughly. Add to the flour mixture with the sugar and currants, and add enough milk to make a stiff dough. Stir all together and put into two greased 7 in. sponge tins. Bake at 425°F (Gas Mark 7) for 15 minutes. Reduce heat to 300°F (Gas Mark 2) and bake for 1 hour. While still warm, sandwich together with 2 oz. butter. Cut up remaining butter, mix with brown sugar and spread on the top. Eat while warm and fresh.

### APPLE GINGERBREAD

1 large cooking apple
6 whole cloves
1 dessertspoon sugar
3 tablespoons water
6 oz. self-raising flour
2 teaspoons ground ginger
3 oz. sugar
1 egg
4 oz. black treacle
3 oz. melted butter

*Icing:*
1 oz. butter
2 oz. black treacle
2 oz. icing sugar
pinch of cinnamon
chopped nuts or crystallised ginger (optional)

Peel, core and slice the apple and put it into a pan with the cloves, 1 dessertspoon sugar and water. Simmer until tender, take out the cloves, and mash the apple with a fork. Leave to cool. Stir together the flour, ginger and 3 oz. sugar. Add the cooked apple, beaten egg, treacle and butter and beat well together. Put into a greased 1½ lb. loaf tin and bake at 350°F (Gas Mark 4) for 40 minutes and cool on a rack.

Cream together the butter, treacle and icing sugar until light and fluffy, and add the cinnamon. Spread on the cake and scatter with chopped nuts or ginger if liked.

### BANANA CAKE

4 oz. butter
4 oz. caster sugar
1 egg
3 bananas
½ teaspoon salt
1 teaspoon bicarbonate of soda
2 tablespoons milk
8 oz. self-raising flour

Cream the butter and sugar until fluffy. Add the beaten egg, mashed bananas and salt and beat to a cream. Stir in the bicarbonate of soda dissolved in the milk, and fold in the flour. Put into a rectangular tin about 7 × 11 in. and bake at 350°F (Gas Mark 4) for 30 minutes. Cool on a wire rack. The cake can be simply dusted with icing sugar. If liked, 2 oz. chopped walnuts, or 2 oz. seedless raisins may be stirred into the cake mixture before baking. For a special occasion, the cake can be finished with a lemon butter icing.

### BANANA AND WALNUT CAKE

8 oz. plain flour
pinch of salt
1 level teaspoon bicarbonate of soda
5 oz. butter
4 oz. caster sugar
3 eggs
2 bananas
1 oz. chopped walnuts
2 tablespoons milk
1 tablespoon lemon juice

Sift the dry ingredients. Cream butter and sugar until light and fluffy, then beat in eggs, one at a time, adding a tablespoon of flour with each. Stir in mashed bananas and nuts, then gently fold in the rest of the flour alternately with the milk and lemon juice. Turn into a well-greased 7 in. square cake tin, lined on the bottom with greaseproof paper. Bake in the centre of a moderate oven at 350°F (Gas Mark 4) for 50-60 minutes or till cake is well risen and firm.

### BLACKBERRY CAKE

4 oz. butter
4 oz. caster sugar
1 egg
8 oz. plain flour
2 teaspoons baking powder
¼ teaspoon salt
¼ pint milk
8 oz. blackberries

*Topping:*
2 oz. butter
4 oz. caster sugar
2 oz. plain flour
½ teaspoon ground cinnamon

Cream together the butter and sugar until light and fluffy, and work in the egg. Gradually add the flour sifted with baking powder and salt, and beat to a smooth batter with the milk. Put into a well-greased 8 in. tin. Wash the blackberries and drain them well. Sprinkle the fruit on the cake batter. Cream together the butter and sugar, flour and cinnamon until the mixture is of crumble consistency. Sprinkle on top of the blackberries and bake at 350°F (Gas Mark 4) for 1 hour.

This may be eaten hot or cold as a pudding with cream or custard, or can be served as a cake. It is best to use a cake tin with a removable bottom so that the cake can be taken out and cooled without disturbing the topping.

### GOOSEBERRY CAKE

12 oz. plain flour
½ teaspoon baking powder
½ teaspoon salt
6 oz. lard
8 oz. gooseberries
3 tablespoons Demerara sugar

Reserve 1 teaspoon of the flour, and sift the rest with the baking powder and salt. Rub in the lard and add enough cold water to make a stiff paste. Roll out into two rounds about 9 in. in diameter. Put one of the rounds on a greased baking sheet and cover with cleaned gooseberries. Sprinkle with sugar and reserved flour. Put on the second round of pastry, wetting the edges to seal them, and press well together with a fork. Bake at 400°F (Gas Mark 6) for 30 minutes. Cool, dust with a little icing sugar and eat cold.

### LEMON CAKE

1½ oz. butter
6 oz. caster sugar
3 egg yolks
¼ teaspoon lemon essence
6 oz. self-raising flour
¼ pint minus two tablespoons milk
pinch of salt

*Icing:*
1 tablespoon grated orange rind
3 tablespoons soft butter
12 oz. icing sugar
2 tablespoons lemon juice
1 tablespoon water
pinch of salt

Cream the butter until light, and gradually add the sugar, egg yolks and lemon essence. When the mixture is soft and fluffy, add the flour alternately with the milk. Add the salt and beat well. Bake in two 8 in. round tins, greased and bottom-lined with greased paper, at 350°F (Gas Mark 4) for 25 minutes. Prepare the icing and ice between the layers, and on the top and sides of the cake.

Make the icing by adding the orange rind to the butter and creaming well. Cream in one-third of the icing sugar with the salt. Mix the lemon juice and water, and add to the mixture alternately with the remaining icing sugar. Beat well until smooth.

### ORANGE JUICE CAKE

4 oz. butter
8 oz. sugar
2 eggs
¼ pint orange juice
8 oz. plain flour
2 teaspoons baking powder
pinch of salt

*Topping:*
3 tablespoons caster sugar
grated rind of 2 oranges

Melt the butter and add the hot butter to the sugar. Beat well, adding the beaten eggs and orange juice. Add the flour sifted with the baking powder and salt, and beat to a smooth batter. Pour into a 7 in. greased tin. Mix together the caster sugar and grated rind and sprinkle on top of the cake. Bake at 350°F (Gas Mark 4) for 1 hour 10 minutes.

### ORANGE LOAF

2 oz. butter
6 oz. caster sugar
1 egg
½ large orange
2 tablespoons milk
7 oz. plain flour
2½ teaspoons baking powder
½ teaspoon salt

Cream the butter and sugar until light and fluffy. Add the

beaten egg gradually with the grated rind and juice of the orange and the milk. Sieve the flour, baking powder and salt, and fold into the creamed mixture. Put into a greased 2 lb. loaf tin, and bake at 375°F (Gas Mark 5) for 1 hour. Cool, slice and spread with butter.

### PLUM CAKE

1 egg
4 oz. caster sugar
4 oz. plain flour
1 teaspoon baking powder
¼ teaspoon salt
4 tablespoons milk
3 tablespoons melted butter
¼ teaspoon lemon essence
1 lb. small eating plums

*Topping:*
2 oz. sugar
1 teaspoon ground cinnamon

Beat the egg and gradually work in the sugar. Add flour sifted with baking powder and salt. Gradually blend in milk, melted butter and essence. Pour into a rectangular tin approximately 7×10 in. Cut the plums in half and arrange face down on the surface, close together. Sprinkle with 4 tablespoons water, sugar and cinnamon. Bake at 350°F (Gas Mark 4) for 45 minutes and serve in squares. This cake can be served warm as a pudding with cream.

### REDCURRANT SLICES

5 oz. butter
8 oz. caster sugar
2 eggs
6 oz. plain flour
1 teaspoon grated lemon rind
12 oz. redcurrants

Cream the butter with 2 oz. sugar and beat in the egg yolks. Fold in the flour and lemon rind which will make a fairly stiff mixture. Spread on to a greased and floured Swiss roll tin. Bake at 375°F (Gas Mark 5) for 20 minutes until golden. Leave on the tin and cool slightly. Cover thickly with the redcurrants. Whisk the egg whites stiffly and fold in 2 oz. sugar. Whisk again until smooth and shiny and fold in 3 oz. sugar. Pile the mixture over the fruit and sprinkle on the remaining sugar. Bake at 250°F (Gas Mark ½) for 30 minutes until the meringue topping sounds hollow if gently tapped. Cool before cutting in slices and taking from the tin.

### FRUIT FRANZIPAN

2 oz. caster sugar
4 oz. butter
8 oz. plain flour
1 egg
2 oz. cake or biscuit crumbs
1 lb. fresh cherries, apricots or eating apples

*Topping:*
2 oz. butter
2 oz. caster sugar
1 egg
1 oz. plain flour
3 oz. ground almonds

*Icing:*
4 tablespoons apricot jam
8 tablespoons icing sugar
1 tablespoon lemon juice

Make pastry by mixing caster sugar, butter, flour and beaten egg. Roll out carefully (this pastry is frail) and line an 8 in. round tin. Sprinkle the cake or biscuit crumbs on top. Stone the cherries or apricots. If using apples, peel and cut in slices, and mix with a few raisins if liked. Put the fruit on top of the crumbs.

Make the topping by creaming together the butter and sugar, working in the egg, flour and almonds. Spread on top of the fruit and bake at 375°F (Gas Mark 5) for 35 minutes. While still warm, brush with a mixture of apricot jam and 1 tablespoon water heated together. Cool and remove from the tin. Mix the icing sugar with the lemon juice and 1 tablespoon water and heat to boiling point. Spread half the mixture on the cake. Leave for a minute or two to set and pour on the remaining icing.

### SOFT FRUIT SHORTCAKE

4 oz. butter
4 oz. caster sugar
2 eggs
grated rind of 1 orange
4 oz. self-raising flour
pinch of salt
1 lb. strawberries, raspberries or currants
½ pint double cream

During the winter, this cake may be made with drained canned fruit such as peaches, apricots or pineapple.

Cream the butter and sugar together. Beat the eggs with the orange rind and add to the fat alternately with the flour sifted with the salt. Mix thoroughly and spread in two greased 7 in. sandwich tins. Bake at 375°F (Gas Mark 5) for 25 minutes. Cool on a rack and sandwich together with lightly crushed fruit and whipped cream. If liked, the cake may be topped with more cream and whole fruit.

(10)

# Jams and Sweet Preserves

Nobody needs vast quantities of boring plum jam, but most people occasionally enjoy a really special jam to spread on bread or toast, on scones, waffles, pancakes or sweet omelettes. A small collection of traditional stillroom preserves can also be useful for emergency cooking, to fill small tarts or flans, to sandwich together plain cakes, to use as a sauce for ice cream, milk or steamed pudding, or to serve in individual portions with a topping of thick cream.

The preserves in this chapter are unusual, and suitable for all these purposes. For preference, put them into small jars which can be used up quickly. Don't make very large quantities at first, but use the odd pound or two of fruit, and aim at a wide variety of preserves in store. Use fresh, just-ripe fruit, and see that it is well-washed and drained. Take away any bruised portions before preparing the fruit for a recipe. Use a large pan so that the preserve does not boil over, as once sugar is dissolved jam must be boiled rapidly to setting point. A test for setting should be made after 5 minutes, and few jams need longer than 20 minutes' boiling. Setting is most easily tested by putting a little jam on to a cold plate. When cool, the surface should wrinkle when pushed with a finger if the jam is ready for potting.

VICTORIAN APPLE MARMALADE

2 lb. eating apples
2 lb. cube sugar
1 teaspoon ground cinnamon

Peel the apples and cut them into thin slices. Put into a stone jar with the sugar and cinnamon, and stand inside a pan of boiling water. Keep the water boiling and shake the jar frequently, but do not stir. When the mixture is smooth and clear, put into small jars, and cover when cold. This can be used in tarts, or is excellent served as an emergency pudding with cream.

### BAUGHURST RECTORY APPLE CHEESE

1 lb. cooking apples
1 lb. caster sugar
3 lemons
4 eggs
4 oz. unsalted butter

Peel the apples and cut them up. Simmer them very gently without water to make a soft pulp. Put the pulp, sugar, grated rind and juice of the lemons and well-beaten eggs into a double saucepan, or a bowl over hot water. Mix very well and add melted butter. Stir over boiling water for 30 minutes and put into jars. Use like lemon curd for tarts or as a spread, and do not keep longer than 2 months.

### BILBERRY JAM

2 lb. bilberries
1½ lb. sugar
juice of 2 lemons

Wash and drain the fruit well. Put it into a bowl with half the sugar and all the lemon juice, cover and leave for 24 hours. Strain the liquid off the berries and put into a preserving pan with the remaining sugar. Heat gently and stir until the sugar has dissolved. Bring to the boil, add the fruit and simmer until the berries are tender. Boil hard for 10 minutes to setting point. Pour into warm jars and cover. This jam is also very good made from frozen bilberries which may be more easily available than the fresh fruit.

### BLACKBERRY AND APPLE CHEESE

2 lb. blackberries
2 lb. cooking apples
sugar

Peel, core and quarter the apples and cook them in ¼ pint water until tender. Add the blackberries and simmer until soft. Put through a fine sieve and measure the pulp. Allow 1 lb. sugar to each pint of pulp, stir until dissolved, and boil until the mixture sets when a little is dropped on to a cold plate. It should be very firm. Put into small straight-sided warm pots, and cover. This may be eaten as a jam, or it can be turned out, sliced and served as a pudding with cream.

### BLACKBERRY AND RHUBARB JAM

4 lb. blackberries
2 lb. rhubarb
¾ pint water
sugar

Simmer blackberries in water until tender and put through a sieve. Cut up rhubarb and put into blackberry pulp. Simmer until soft. Weigh the fruit and add 1 lb. sugar to each pound of pulp. Stir in sugar until dissolved, then boil hard to setting point. Pour into hot jars and cover.

### CRANBERRY CONSERVE

1 lb. cranberries
4 oz. raisins
1½ lb. sugar
1 orange
8 oz. walnut kernels

Wash the cranberries and put them into a saucepan with ¼ pint cold water, and boil until the skins break. Sieve and return the pulp to a saucepan. Add 4 tablespoons boiling water, raisins and sugar. Cut the flesh of the orange into very small pieces and add to the mixture. Bring to boiling point and simmer for 20 minutes. Add chopped walnuts, cool and fill jars. This makes a delicious tart filling.

### CRANBERRY AND APPLE JELLY

3 lb. cooking apples or crab apples
sugar
8 oz. cranberries
lemon juice

Wash the apples and cut them up roughly, including the peel and pips. Cook with 1½ pints water until pulped. Put through a jelly bag until the liquid stops dripping. Measure the juice and allow 1 lb. sugar to each pint. Add the cranberries and 1 dessertspoon lemon juice to each pint of juice.

Boil rapidly for about 10 minutes until setting point is reached. Put into small warm jars and cover when cold. This is a firm, slightly tart jelly which is excellent with roast meat or poultry.

GOOSEBERRY, APPLE AND GINGER JELLY

3 lb. cooking apples
3 lb. gooseberries
3¼ pints water
1 piece root ginger
6½ lb. sugar
1 bottle liquid pectin
green vegetable colouring (optional)

Cut the apples into small pieces, but do not peel or core them. Wash the gooseberries without topping or tailing them. Put the gooseberries and apples into a large saucepan with the water and ginger and simmer covered for 20 minutes or until the fruit is soft enough to crush. Strain through a jelly bag and measure the juice into a pan. If necessary make up to 4 pints with water. Add the sugar and heat gently, stirring occasionally, until the sugar has dissolved. Stir in the pectin, bring to a full rolling boil and boil rapidly for 1 minute. Remove from heat, skim, and stir in the colouring if desired. Put into small jars and cover.

GRAPE JAM

4 lb. small green seedless grapes
1 lb. cooking apples
3¾ lb. sugar

Remove the stalks from the grapes. Peel, core and slice the apples. Put the sugar into a pan with 1 pint water and simmer gently until the sugar has dissolved. Add the grapes and apples and boil until the mixture sets when tested on a cold plate. Pour into jars and cover at once. This is very good for a tart filling.

LEMON AND APPLE MARMALADE

3 lemons
3 lb. cooking apples
4¾ lb. sugar

Slice the lemons and soak them overnight in 3 pints cold water. Simmer in the water until the lemon rind is tender. Peel the apples and slice them. Add to the lemon mixture and simmer until tender. Stir in the sugar until dissolved and boil to setting point. Put into jars and cover when cold.

### LEMON MINCEMEAT

3 large lemons
3 large cooking apples
1 lb. stoned raisins
8 oz. currants
1 lb. shredded suet
8 oz. sugar
4 oz. chopped mixed peel
2 tablespoons bitter orange marmalade
¼ pint brandy

Grate the lemon rinds and squeeze out the juice. Remove the pith from the lemon peel, and then boil the peel until very tender. Put through the mincer. Bake the apples, and remove the skin. Mash the apple pulp and mix with the lemon peel, dried fruit, suet, sugar, mixed peel, marmalade and brandy. Put into jars and cover tightly and keep for 2 weeks before using.

### MEDLAR JELLY

2 lb. medlars
sugar
1 lemon

Peel very ripe medlars, remove the pips, and slice the flesh into a pan with enough water to cover the fruit. Simmer with the cut-up lemon until soft. Strain the juice through a jelly bag. Allow 12 oz. sugar to each pint of juice and stir until dissolved. Boil fast for 10 minutes until transparent. Skim well and cool slightly before pouring into jars. This can be eaten with bread and butter, or served with game.

### MULBERRY AND APPLE JAM

3 lb. mulberries
1 lb. cooking apples

1 pint water
¼ oz. citric acid
3 lb. sugar

Rinse the mulberries. Peel and cut up the apples. Cook the fruit in water with the acid until pulpy. Stir in the sugar until dissolved and boil to setting point. Pour into hot jars and cover.

### PEACH CONSERVE

2 lb. peaches
1½ lb. sugar
2 teaspoons orange flower water
2 teaspoons rosewater

Dip the ripe peaches in boiling water and rub off skins. Take out the stones and break the stones to remove the kernels. Put the fruit into a preserving pan and sprinkle with the sugar. Add the kernels, orange flower water and rosewater, and cook on a low heat until the sugar has dissolved. Bring to the boil and cook for 5 minutes. Put into small warm jars. This is delicious to eat on toast, and it can be used as a sauce over vanilla ice cream.

### PEACH MARMALADE

8 large ripe peaches
1 orange
sugar

Peel the peaches and remove the stones. Put the peaches and the unpeeled orange through a fine mincer. Weigh the pulp and add the same weight of sugar. Stir over low heat until the sugar has dissolved and continue simmering until thick. Put into small jars and cover.

### PEAR AND PINEAPPLE JAM

3 lb. eating pears
1 small fresh pineapple
5 lemons
4 lb. sugar
miniature bottle of Kirsch, or 3 tablespoonfuls

Peel and core the pears and cut them into small pieces. Peel the pineapple and chop it finely. Put pears, pineapple and grated rind and juice of the lemons into a pan and simmer for 10 minutes. Stir in the sugar until dissolved, then boil hard to setting point. Stir in the Kirsch and reheat without boiling. Pour into hot jars and cover.

### PLUM GUMBO

5 lb. plums
2 lb. seedless raisins
3 oranges
5 lb. sugar

Cut the plums into small pieces and put into a preserving pan. Add the raisins and the unpeeled oranges cut in thin crosswise slices. Add the sugar and bring slowly to boiling point, stirring occasionally to dissolve the sugar. Simmer to the consistency of marmalade. Cool slightly, stir well, and fill jars. This can be used as a spread or tart filling, or can be eaten as a pudding with cream.

### QUINCE JELLY

4 lb. quinces
6 pints water
sugar

Wash the quinces and cut them up finely without peeling. Simmer in a pan with 4 pints water and the lid on for about 1 hour. Strain the liquid. Add the remaining water to the pulp and simmer for 30 minutes, then strain. Mix both strained liquids and allow 1 lb. sugar to each pint. Bring the juice to the boil, stir in the sugar and bring back to the boil. Boil rapidly to setting point, skim, pot and cover.

### QUINCE AND LEMON MARMALADE

1½ lb. quinces
2 lemons
1 pint water
3 lb. sugar

Peel and core the quinces, and cut the flesh into slices. Put into a pan with the juice of the lemons, the finely shredded lemon peel and the water. Put the cores and peel of the quinces into a muslin bag and hang it in the saucepan. Simmer slowly for 45 minutes. Stir in warm sugar until dissolved, and boil rapidly to setting point. Remove the muslin bag. Leave marmalade to cool for a few minutes, stir well, and pour into pots.

### RASPBERRY AND PEACH JAM

2 lb. peaches
2 lb. raspberries
¼ pint water
3 lb. sugar

Peel and stone the peaches and cut them into pieces. Crack some of the stones, and put the kernels with the peaches into the water. Simmer until tender. Stir in the raspberries and sugar, and when the sugar has dissolved, boil hard to setting point. Pour into hot jars and cover. Yield 5-6 lbs.

### RHUBARB MARMALADE

4 lb. rhubarb
5 lb. sugar
grated rind of 1 lemon
juice of 2 oranges
1 teaspoon ground cinnamon
½ teaspoon ground cloves
1 lb. seedless raisins

Wash and peel the rhubarb and cut it into 1 in. pieces. Cover with sugar and leave to stand overnight. Stir in the lemon rind, orange juice, spices and raisins. Bring to the boil and simmer for 40 minutes until the mixture is thick. Put into jars and cover. This makes a delicious filling for small tarts.

### FOUR FRUIT JELLY

1 lb. redcurrants
1 lb. raspberries
1 lb. strawberries
1 lb. black cherries
1 teaspoon tartaric acid
1 pint water
sugar

Use firm fruit which is just ripe. Put all the fruit into a pan with the acid and water. Simmer until the fruit is soft. Strain through a jelly bag and measure the juice. Allow 1 lb. sugar to each pint of juice. Heat the juice gently, stirring in the sugar until dissolved. Boil hard to setting point and pour into hot jars. This jelly is very good for pastries and tarts.

### FOUR FRUIT MARMALADE

2 cooking apples
2 sweet oranges
2 lemons
1 grapefruit
sugar

Peel and core the apples. Cut the oranges, lemons and grapefruit in half and take out pips. Put the apple peel, cores and fruit pips into a muslin bag. Chop the apples and shred the citrus fruit finely. Weigh the fruit and allow 1 pint water to each pound of fruit. Put fruit, water and bag of pips into the pan and boil gently for 1½ hours. Take out the bag of pips and squeeze out the liquid. Measure the fruit mixture and allow 1 lb. sugar to each pint of pulp. Warm the sugar and add to the fruit. Stir until dissolved and then boil rapidly to setting point. Cool slightly and stir well. Pour into hot jars and cover.

### GOLDEN CURD

2 oz. butter
2 oranges
1 lemon
8 oz. sugar
4 eggs

Melt the butter in the top of a double saucepan. Grate the orange and lemon rinds finely, and squeeze out the juice. Put the juice through a strainer. Add grated rinds, juice and sugar to the butter and stir until the sugar dissolves. Cool slightly and stir in the well-beaten eggs. Return to the heat and cook gently, stirring until the mixture thickens and coats the back of a spoon, which will take about 10 minutes. Pour into hot jars and cover. This will keep for 1 month.

SUMMER HARLEQUIN

1 lb. cherries
1 lb. redcurrants
2 oranges
8-oz. can pineapple
1 lb. raspberries
sugar

Stone the cherries and stem the currants. Cut the oranges in half, remove the pips and cores, and slice the oranges very thinly. Drain the pineapple and cut into small pieces. Mix all the fruit and allow 1 lb. sugar to each lb. of fruit. Put the fruit and pineapple syrup into a pan and simmer gently for 1 hour. Add the sugar and stir gently until dissolved. Boil to setting point, pour into small jars and cover. This is delicious in tarts and sponge cakes, or can be used as a sauce with ice cream.

APPLE GINGER

4 lb. eating apples
4 lb. sugar
3 pints water
2 oz. ground ginger

Peel and core the apples and cut them into thin slices. Dissolve the sugar in the water and boil the syrup until thick. Add the apple slices and boil until transparent. Stir in ginger, boil for 5 minutes, pour into jars and cover. This is a traditional recipe which is very good for filling tarts.

APPLES IN WINE

8 lemons
1 pint white wine
4½ lb. sugar
5 lb. eating apples
2 tablespoons brandy

Peel the lemons thinly and pour on 1 pint boiling water, and the wine. Leave for 30 minutes. Put lemon peel and liquid into a pan with the juice of the lemons and the sugar. Boil for 10 minutes. Strain the liquid and return to the pan.

Peel and core the apples, and cut into slices. Simmer until the apples are soft and the syrup is thick. Stir in brandy, heat and pour into hot screw-top jars. This is very good served with cream.

### TIPSY APRICOTS

8 oz. dried apricots
1 pint boiling water
1 lb. granulated sugar
¼ pint cold water
12 tablespoons gin or brandy

Put the apricots into a bowl, pour on the boiling water, and leave to soak overnight. Drain the fruit, and chop roughly. Dissolve the sugar in the cold water over a gentle heat. Add the apricots and bring to the boil. Simmer for 15 minutes. Leave for 2 hours until cold. Stir in gin or brandy, and store in screw-top jars. This makes a delicious filling for cakes or pastry cases, or it can be used as a sauce for ices or puddings.

### ROLLING CHERRIES

3 lb. Morello cherries
1 lb. caster sugar

Put the cherries and sugar in layers into a large preserving jar and cover tightly. Roll the jar to and fro for a short time every day for six weeks and store in a cool place. This recipe dates from 1832, and cherries taste as if they have been preserved in brandy.

### PRESERVED ORANGES

1 lb. thin-skinned oranges
1 lb. sugar

Cut the oranges in half and remove the seeds. If the oranges are very small, they may be kept whole. Score the peel with a sharp knife, without cutting through. Soak the fruit for 3 days in cold water, changing the water night and morning. Tie the whole or half oranges into a piece of cloth and boil them until a skewer will slip into the skin easily. Mix the sugar with ½ pint of the liquid in which the fruit has been cooked. Simmer together for 10 minutes. Strain this syrup through a cloth, add the oranges and cook until the syrup will set into jelly when a little is tested on a cold plate. The oranges should be turned several times while simmering, so that they cook evenly. Pack the oranges into wide-mouthed preserving jars, pour over the syrup and seal tightly. These are delicious if the oranges are cut in quarters before serving, covered with the syrup and finished with thick cream flavoured with a little brandy or liqueur.

### BRANDIED PEACHES

10 lb. small ripe peaches
3 lb. caster sugar
1 bottle brandy

Peel, halve and stone the peaches. Crack the stones and remove the kernels. Pack the peaches and kernels into preserving jars, sprinkling thickly between the layers with sugar. Fill up with brandy, seal tightly and store at least a month before using. Two lb. jars will hold about six small peaches, and this recipe will make about six jars of fruit, enough for six dinner parties. This means the recipe is not necessarily extravagant, and the fruit will store for years.

### STRAWBERRIES IN SYRUP

2 lb. strawberries
2 lb. sugar

Hull the strawberries and arrange in alternate layers with sugar in a bowl. Leave for 24 hours and boil for 5 minutes. Leave for another 24 hours and boil for 5 minutes. Leave for a further 24 hours and boil for 7 minutes. Put into small warm jars and seal. This preserve has a full flavour, and is excellent with puddings and ices.

### STRAWBERRY AND ALMOND BUTTER

8 oz. unsalted butter
1 lb. icing sugar
1 lb. strawberries
2 oz. almond kernels
pinch of salt

Cream the butter and icing sugar until light and fluffy. Sieve the strawberries and work the purée into the butter mixture. Add the finely chopped almonds and salt. Put into a jar, cover and keep in the refrigerator. This is delicious on toast, waffles or pancakes.

(11)

# Spiced Fruits, Chutneys and Sauces

Small quantities of fruit can be conveniently turned into spiced fruits and chutneys to accompany meat, poultry and fish. Made with fruit, these relishes are less coarse than those made with vegetables, and for this reason they are best made with cider or wine vinegar, or with distilled white vinegar, rather than with the common brown malt vinegar. Spiced fruits are best made with whole spices so that the accompanying syrup remains clear; chutneys may be made with ground spices. White sugar is best for spiced fruit in syrup, but brown sugar may be used for chutney to give added colour and rich flavour.

Chutney should be cooked until thick and brown, and about the consistency of jam. It should be packed into jars which can be tightly sealed with a screwtop. If a metal top is used, it should be lined with an acid-resistant disc so that there is no reaction between metal and vinegar. A paper covering, however thick, will result in the chutney drying out. Chutneys are best packed in small jars so that each one remains fresh and moist when opened. Spiced fruits can be packed in preserving jars, or in screwtop honey or coffee jars. Both kinds of preserve are particularly delicious with cold ham, pork or poultry, and sweet chutney is a fitting complement to curry or well-spiced dishes.

SPICED APRICOTS

1 lb. dried apricots
½ oz. whole cloves
½ in. cinnamon stick
½ oz. whole allspice
1½ pints white vinegar
1¼ lb. sugar

Soak the apricots in cold water overnight. Put the spices in a muslin bag and bring to the boil with the vinegar. Add the drained apricots to the vinegar and simmer for 5 minutes. Spoon the apricots into warm jars. Add the sugar to the vinegar, bring to the boil, and continue boiling for 5 minutes until the mixture is syrupy. Remove the spice bag, pour the syrup over the fruit, and seal tightly. This is a good preserve to eat with ham or pork.

SPICED BLACKBERRIES

½ pint cider vinegar
¼ oz. allspice
¼ oz. coriander
¼ oz. cardomums
½ oz. cinnamon
1 bay leaf
1 lb. sugar
2½ lb. blackberries
2 rose geranium leaves

Simmer together vinegar, allspice, coriander, cardomums, cinnamon and bay leaf. Bring to the boil and then take off heat, and leave the spices to infuse for two or three hours. Take out the spices and bayleaf, and gently reheat the vinegar and the sugar until the sugar has dissolved. Wash the blackberries and add them, together with the rose geranium leaves. Simmer gently for five minutes until the fruit is tender. Take out the rose geranium leaves. Lift out the fruit, drain and put into warm preserving jars. Boil the vinegar until it becomes syrupy, pour over the blackberries and seal tightly while hot. This is very good served with cold meat or poultry.

SPICED CRANBERRIES

4 lb. cranberries
¾ pint cider vinegar
3 lb. sugar
2 tablespoons ground cinnamon
1 tablespoon ground cloves
1 tablespoon ground allspice

Use a thick saucepan, and put in all the ingredients together with ¼ pint water. Cook over a low heat for 45 minutes, stirring well. Put into small hot jars and cover.

SWEET SPICED DAMSONS

4 lb. large ripe damsons
1 pint vinegar
1½ lb. sugar
1 oz. mixed pickling spice

Prick the damsons with a large needle. Put the vinegar, sugar and spice into a pan and heat until the sugar is dissolved. Add the damsons, cook until soft but not broken, and then lift carefully into jars. Reduce the vinegar to a syrup by boiling, remove the spices, and pour over the fruit. Cover tightly. These are delicious with cold poultry and meat.

SPICED GOOSEBERRIES

3 lb. gooseberries
1¼ lb. sugar
½ pint vinegar
¼ oz. ground cloves

Top and tail the gooseberries and chop them roughly. Put into a pan with the sugar, vinegar and cloves. Cook gently until the sugar has dissolved. Bring to the boil, then continue simmering, stirring well for 45 minutes. Pour into jars and cover when cold.

SPICED MELON

4 lb. melon
2 oz. salt
1 pint water
1 lb. sugar
1 pint vinegar
8 whole cloves
1 in. cinnamon stick

Peel the melon and cut the flesh into ½ in. cubes. Stir the salt into the water until dissolved, put in the melon and leave overnight. Drain off the salt water and cover the melon with fresh water. Bring to the boil, and then simmer until the melon cubes are tender and clear. Put the sugar, vinegar and spices into a pan and boil for 20 minutes until syrupy.

Strain the syrup and bring to the boil. Add the drained melon and boil for 10 minutes. Put into preserving jars and cover tightly at once. Serve with ham or chicken.

### SPICED ORANGE RINGS

6 thin-skinned oranges
¾ pint white vinegar
12 oz. sugar
2 teaspoons whole cloves
3 in. cinnamon stick

Wipe the oranges but do not peel them. Slice across in ¼ in. rounds. Put into a pan with water to cover and simmer for 45 minutes until the rings are tender. Put the vinegar, sugar and spices into another pan and bring to the boil. Drain the rings and simmer them in the vinegar syrup a few at a time. Cook gently until the rind is clear. Put the fruit into hot preserving jars. Boil the syrup until it starts to thicken and pour it over the fruit to cover completely. Put a few of the cloves into each jar and seal tightly. Serve with ham or poultry.

### PICKLED PEACHES

1¾ lb. sugar
1 pint white vinegar
1 oz. whole cloves
1 oz. whole allspice
1 oz. cinnamon stick
3½ lb. peaches

Dissolve the sugar in the vinegar on a very low heat. Put the spice into a muslin bag and put into the vinegar. Bring to the boil and put in the peeled peaches cut in quarters. Simmer until tender but not soft. Drain the fruit and pack into preserving jars to within 1 in. of the tops. Boil the vinegar until syrupy, remove spices, and pour over the fruit. Seal tightly. These peaches are delicious with ham, pork or poultry.

### SPICED PEARS

2 lb. small cooking pears
2 teaspoons whole cloves
8 oz. sugar

½ pint white vinegar
piece of lemon rind
piece of root ginger
1 in. cinnamon stick
2 teaspoons whole allspice

Peel and core the pears and cut them in half. Stick a clove into each piece of pear. Dissolve the sugar in the vinegar and put the lemon rind and spices into a piece of muslin suspended in the pan. Simmer the pears in this mixture until they are tender and begin to look transparent. Pack in clean hot jars. Boil the syrup until it starts to thicken slightly and pour over the pears. Seal tightly.

SPICED PINEAPPLE

1 large ripe pineapple
½ pint cider vinegar
8 oz. sugar
1 teaspoon ground cinnamon
1 teaspoon ground cloves
1 teaspoon ground ginger
1 tablespoon curry powder

Peel and core the pineapple and cut the flesh into small chunks, keeping any juice which runs out. Mix the juice, vinegar and sugar and bring to the boil. Add the spices and simmer for 5 minutes. Add the pineapple and cook for 5 minutes. Pour into hot jars and cover tightly.

SPICED PICKLED PLUMS

1 pint white vinegar
1 oz. cinnamon stick
¼ oz. mixed pickling spice
¼ oz. allspice berries
2 lb. sugar
2 lb. Victoria plums

Boil together the vinegar, spices and sugar until the liquid is thick and syrupy. Wipe the plums, cut them into halves, and remove the stones. Prick the plum halves well with a needle and put them into preserving jars. Pour over the cool syrup.

Next day, strain off the syrup, reboil, cool and pour over the fruit again. When cold, cover and store for at least 3 months before using.

### SPICED PRUNES

1 lb. large prunes
cold tea
1 pint vinegar
1 lb. sugar
1 in. stick cinnamon
1 teaspoon whole cloves
10 whole allspice
1 blade mace

Cover prunes with tea and soak overnight. In the morning, simmer the prunes in the tea until plump and tender. Boil together vinegar and sugar with the spices in a muslin bag, then add the prunes and cooking liquid. Simmer for 5 minutes. Lift out prunes and put into preserving jars. Boil up the syrup, pour over the prunes, and seal at once. These are very good with pork, duck or goose.

### SPICED RHUBARB

4 lb. rhubarb
3 lb. brown sugar
½ pint vinegar
1 orange
2 lemons
½ oz. whole allspice
½ oz. whole cloves
1 cinnamon stick

Clean the rhubarb and cut it in small pieces. Put into a preserving pan with the sugar and vinegar, and the juice and grated rind of the orange and lemons. Tie the spices into a piece of muslin and add to the pan. Heat gradually, stirring well until the mixture boils. Simmer gently, stirring frequently, until the mixture thickens. Take out the spice bag, put rhubarb into jars and cover.

### NORFOLK APPLE CHUTNEY

4 lb. cooking apples
2 lb. Demerara sugar
4 pints vinegar
4 oz. mustard seed
2 teaspoons ground ginger
4 oz. salt
1½ lb. sultanas
½ oz. garlic
½ oz. cayenne pepper

Peel and core the apples and cut them into pieces. Put into a pan with the sugar and vinegar and cook to a pulp. Put into a jar with the mustard seed, ginger, salt, sultanas, crushed garlic and cayenne pepper. Stir every day for a week and then put into jars.

### KING'S CHUTNEY

1½ lb. cooking apples
8 oz. crystallised ginger
½ oz. mustard powder
12 oz. Demerara sugar
6 teaspoons salt
1 teaspoon ground ginger
½ teaspoon cayenne pepper
1 teaspoon pepper
8 oz. stoned raisins
4 oz. sultanas
4 oz. onions
1 pint vinegar

Peel and chop the apples and chop the ginger. Put into a casserole with all the other ingredients including finely chopped onions. Cover and cook at 325°F (Gas Mark 3) for 4 hours, stirring occasionally. Put into jars and cover.

### APRICOT CHUTNEY

1 lb. dried apricots
1 garlic clove
3 peppercorns
4 oz. sultanas

8 oz. sugar
1 orange
½ pint white vinegar

Chop the apricots and soak them overnight. Drain off the soaking liquid. Put the fruit into a pan with the chopped garlic clove, peppercorns, sultanas and sugar. Add the grated rind and juice of the orange. Bring to the boil and add the vinegar, and simmer until the chutney is thick, in about 45 minutes. Put into small hot jars.

BANANA CHUTNEY

6 bananas
½ pint vinegar
4 oz. brown sugar
3 oz. sultanas
½ oz. curry powder
½ teaspoon ground cinnamon
1 tablespoon salt

Peel and cut up the bananas and boil them in the vinegar to a pulp. Stir in the sugar until it dissolves, and leave to cool. Chop the sultanas and add them to the bananas together with the spices and salt. Stir together well and leave to stand for 12 hours. Put into jars and cover.

BLACKBERRY CHUTNEY

6 lb. blackberries
2 lb. cooking apples
2 lb. onions
1 oz. salt
2 oz. mustard
2 oz. ground ginger
2 teaspoons ground mace
1 teaspoon cayenne pepper
2 pints vinegar
2 lb. brown sugar

Wash the blackberries and put into a pan with peeled and chopped apples, chopped onions, salt, spices and vinegar. Simmer gently for 1 hour, stirring well. Put through a sieve and return purée to the pan. Add the sugar, stir gently to dissolve and cook for 20 minutes until thick. Put into small pots and cover.

### CHERRY CHUTNEY

1½ lb. black eating cherries
4 oz. seedless raisins
4 tablespoons honey
4 tablespoons brown sugar
2 teaspoons ground mixed spice
¼ pint white vinegar

Take the stones out of the cherries, saving any juice which runs from the fruit. Put the cherries, juice, raisins, honey, sugar, spice and vinegar into a heavy pan and simmer gently until the sugar has melted. Bring to the boil and boil for 5 minutes, then simmer for 30 minutes, stirring well. Put into small jars and seal tightly. This is excellent with ham or poultry.

### ELDERBERRY CHUTNEY

1 lb. elderberries
½ pint vinegar
1 onion
2 oz. brown sugar
½ teaspoon ground allspice
½ teaspoon salt
½ teaspoon mustard powder

Remove the berries from stems and mash them to a pulp. Put into a pan with the vinegar, chopped onion, sugar, allspice, salt and mustard. Bring to the boil, then simmer while stirring frequently until the mixture is thick. Put into jars and cover.

### GREEN FIG CHUTNEY

2 lb. green figs
1 lb. onions
4 oz. crystallised ginger
1 pint vinegar
8 oz. brown sugar
2 teaspoons salt
½ teaspoon pepper

Cut up the figs, onions and crystallised ginger into small pieces. Boil together the vinegar, sugar, salt and pepper. Add the remaining ingredients and bring back to the boil. Simmer for 45 minutes until the mixture is thick. Put into jars and cover.

### GOOSEBERRY CHUTNEY

3 lb. hard gooseberries
3 onions
8 oz. sultanas
12 oz. Demerara sugar
1½ pints white vinegar
2 teaspoons mustard powder
1 teaspoon turmeric
1 teaspoon ground ginger
salt and pepper
nutmeg

Top and tail the gooseberries and put through a coarse mincer with the onions. Add the sultanas, sugar, vinegar, mustard, turmeric and ginger, with a pinch each of salt, pepper and nutmeg. Simmer for 2 hours over a low heat. Put into jars, cover well and keep for 1 month before using.

### LEMON CHUTNEY

3 lemons
8 oz. onions
1 oz. salt
4 oz. stoned raisins
12 oz. brown sugar
1 pint vinegar
pinch of cayenne pepper

Slice the lemons, removing the pips, and slice the onions. Put into a dish and sprinkle with salt. Leave for 24 hours and put into a pan with the raisins, sugar, vinegar and cayenne pepper. Stir until the mixture reaches boiling point, then simmer for 45 minutes. Put into jars and cover when cold.

ORANGE CHUTNEY

6 oranges
1 lb. stoned dates
8 oz. onions
1 dessertspoon ground ginger
1 dessertspoon salt
1 pint vinegar

Peel the oranges, remove the pips, and cut into thin slices. Cut the dates in half and chop the onions finely. Put all the ingredients together in a pan and simmer gently for 1 hour until thick. Put into small jars and seal tightly.

PEAR CHUTNEY

3½ lb. ripe pears
2 oranges
1 teaspoon ground cloves
1 teaspoon ground cinnamon
1 teaspoon ground allspice
1 lb. seedless raisins
1½ lb. sugar
½ pint white vinegar

Peel and core the pears and chop the flesh. Put into a pan with the grated orange rind and juice, spices, raisins, sugar and vinegar. Bring to the boil, then reduce heat and simmer for 2 hours, stirring well. Pour into warm jars and seal tightly.

PLUM CHUTNEY

2½ lb. plums
1 lb. carrots
1 pint vinegar
1 lb. raisins
1 lb. soft brown sugar
1 oz. garlic
1 oz. chillies
1 oz. ground ginger
1½ oz. salt

Stone the plums and mince the carrots. Add them to the

vinegar and simmer until soft. Add the raisins, sugar, chopped garlic and chillies, ginger and salt. Simmer for 1 hour until the mixture is thick, put into jars and cover tightly.

### SUSSEX RHUBARB CHUTNEY

2 lb. rhubarb
8 oz. onions
1½ lb. brown sugar
8 oz. sultanas
1 teaspoon mustard powder
1 teaspoon pepper
1 teaspoon ground mixed spice
1 teaspoon ground ginger
1 teaspoon salt
¼ teaspoon cayenne pepper
1 pint vinegar

Cut the rhubarb into 1 in. lengths. Chop the onions finely. Put all the ingredients into a heavy pan and simmer gently, stirring frequently for about 2 hours, until the mixture is of the consistency of jam. Put into jars and seal tightly.

### UNCOOKED FRUIT RELISH

1 lb. cooking apples
8 oz. onions
1 green pepper
2 oz. dates
4 oz. sultanas
1 teaspoon ground ginger
2 tablespoons white wine vinegar
1 teaspoon salt

Peel and core the apples, and peel the onions. Mince together the apples, onions, pepper, dates and sultanas. Add the ginger, vinegar and salt. Mix well, put into small jars and cover. Store in a cool place and use within six weeks.

PLUM SAUCE

4 lb. plums or damsons
8 oz. onions
1 pint vinegar
1 oz. salt
½ oz. ground ginger
½ oz. ground allspice
½ oz. ground nutmeg
½ oz. mustard powder
8 oz. sugar

Cut up the fruit and onions and cook in the vinegar with the salt and spices for 30 minutes. Put through a sieve, stir in the sugar, and bring to the boil. Simmer for 1 hour, stirring occasionally, and bottle while still warm. This is a good way of using up windfalls, or mixtures of odd plums and damsons which are not good enough for table use.

(12)

# Drying, Bottling, Freezing, Crystallising and Syrups

When plenty of fruit is available it is well worth preserving in a variety of ways for future use. As well as garden fruit, it is worth buying imported fruit such as pineapples when they are in season to give sparkle to otherwise simple meals. Although most people are now aware of the value of a freezer for preserving fruit, there are many traditional ways of keeping produce which can be tried successfully.

*Storing apples and pears*

Apples and pears can be stored in houses and sheds, and it is generally unnecessary to freeze or bottle them. Apples which ripen latest tend to store best—ripeness can be tested by lifting an apple gently on its stalk on the tree branch. If it comes off easily into the hand, the apple is ripe. Do not put apples into store immediately after picking, but let them cool and sweat in an airy place first, which should be dark and slightly moist. Keep separate the different varieties with varying keeping qualities, and store them in trays in a frost-proof shed, cellar or attic. Greengrocers' boxes which can be stacked with space between are useful for storage. Special eating apples can be wrapped individually in sheets of newspaper and stored in boxes. Pears tend to ripen suddenly, so they should be inspected regularly, and any unsound fruit removed at once.

*Drying fruit*

Drying is the oldest method of preservation, and fruit used to be dried in the sun after a short blanching in boiling water. This is not always convenient, and it is better to dry fruit in the house. Apples, pears, grapes, cherries, plums, apricots, peaches and grapes may all be treated by this method, and take up little storage space as their weight and bulk is considerably reduced by drying.

Fruit may be dried in an oven, a warm cupboard or a rack over a stove, in a constant gentle heat with a current of air to carry away moisture (this is best obtained by leaving the cupboard or oven door slightly open). Heat may be used after a baking session. Spread out the fruit on oven racks or wire cake trays covered with muslin which should be scalded before use to prevent scorching. The ideal heat for drying is between 120°F-150°F as the fruit should be dried, not cooked or scorched.

### APPLE RINGS AND PEARS

Apples should be ripe but not over-ripe. Use a silver or stainless steel knife to peel and core the apples and cut them into rings about ¼ in. thick. Put into a basin of salt water at once (½ oz. salt to 1 quart water) and leave for 10 minutes. Thread the rings on a stick which can rest on the runners of an oven; the rings should not touch each other. Dry at 150°F for 6-7 hours, so that the apples are like dry chamois leather, moist and pliable. Cool in the air before packing tightly in paper bags, or in dry jars or tins, and store in a dry dark place.

Pears can be dried in halves or quarters placed on racks, but the juicy varieties are difficult to handle.

Soak the fruit for 24 hours before cooking, and use the soaking water for cooking.

### CHERRIES

Take off stalks and remove stones. Dry on trays for about 3 hours, but remove from the heat if there is any sign of the colour changing.

### GRAPES

Use fully ripe fruit and whole dry grapes. Spread out in a single layer and test by squeezing. No moisture will appear when the grapes are ready.

### PEACHES AND APRICOTS

Use ripe fruit, cut in half and remove stones. Put on trays, cut side up. Change the position of the fruit occasionally, and press flat from time to time as fruit dries.

### PLUMS

Use ripe fruit and dry whole or halved and stoned. Dry slowly to the texture of prunes.

NORMANDY PIPPINS
small even-sized pippin apples
water

Bring a large pan of water to the boil and throw in clean unpeeled apples. Leave until cold. Throw the fruit into fresh boiling water, take out and peel, but leave the stalks on. Put the apples on a wire rack in a very low oven (275°F or Gas Mark 1). As the apples get soft, press them between the hands and return to the oven until they are dry and leathery. Cool and pack in boxes. To serve, soak in a rich sugar-and-water syrup and serve when they are soft. The bottom oven of a solid fuel cooker is useful for this drying process.

A similar method was traditional for Norfolk Biffins (Beaufin apples), and they were prepared in a low oven between clean straw.

*Bottling fruit*

While fruit bottling has been largely superseded by freezing, it is still often convenient to prepare bottles of fruit by one of four methods. Fruit purées are particularly useful for later use, and attractive mixtures of fruit can be bottled together such as currants, gooseberries and raspberries.

PRESERVING: OVEN METHOD

Wash and drain the jars and lids. Pack tightly with the prepared fruit to the top of the jar. Place in a very slow oven on a piece of cardboard or several thicknesses of paper as insulation against the intense heat. The jars should be covered with the lids, to prevent the fruit from charring. Leave in the oven about 45-60 minutes until the fruit appears cooked and has shrunk a little. Remove the jars one at a time, place them on a mat or folded newspaper and cover the fruit with boiling water. Seal immediately with rubber ring, lid and clip or screw-band. As the jars cool, the screw-bands will need further tightening. Test next day. Remove the screw-band or clip; if the seal is perfect, it should be possible to lift the jar by the lid. If the lid comes off, the seal is imperfect and the fruit should be eaten within a few days or re-sterilised. Store in a cool, dark place. Remove screw-band or clip which may rust if left on the jar. Grease and store them for future use.

### PRESERVING IN A DEEP PAN

Wash and drain the jars and lids. Pack the jars tightly with the prepared fruit. Apples and pears should be peeled with a stainless knife and put immediately into brine; use 1 teaspoon of salt to 1 pint of water and pack into the jars after rinsing. Shake soft, juicy fruits down; for hard fruits the handle of a wooden spoon is useful for arranging the fruit in layers and for packing tightly. Pack the fruit almost to the top of the jar. Cover the fruit with cold water, filling the jars to overflowing. When the screw-band is used, it should be given a half-turn back to allow for expansion. Put some straw, newspaper, or cloth in the bottom of a deep pan or steriliser; place in the jars and completely cover with cold water. A large fish kettle, bucket or any container which is deep enough can be used. The jars should not touch each other or the sides of the container. Bring the water slowly to simmering point. This should take 1½ hours, then maintain at this temperature for 15 minutes; pears require 30 minutes.

Remove the jars one at a time from the steriliser; place on a wooden table or board and tighten the screw-bands. As the jars cool, the screw-band will need further tightening. Test the next day. Remove the screw-band; if the seal is perfect, it should be possible to lift the jar by the lid. If the lid comes off, the seal is imperfect and the fruit should be eaten within a few days or re-sterilised. Store in a cool, dark place. Remove the screw-band which may rust if left on the jar. Grease and store them for future use.

### PULPING

This is a simple way of bottling stewed fruit, whether soft or hard. Windfall apples or bruised plums can be bottled by this method if all the bruised parts are removed first. Apples and pears should be peeled with a stainless knife and put immediately into brine; use 1 teaspoon salt to 1 pint water. Stew the fruit in a little water until thoroughly pulped; only enough water is needed to prevent the pan from burning. About 30 minutes' stewing is needed for soft fruit—longer for hard-textured fruit. Pour at once into hot, clean jars. Seal immediately and when screw-band is used, give a half-turn back to allow for expansion. Place the jars in a pan of hot water on a false bottom of straw, newspaper or cloth, bring to the boil and boil for 5 minutes. The jars should be completely covered with water. Remove, then tighten screw-band. As the jars cool, the screw-bands will need further tightening. Test next day. Remove screw-band; if the seal is perfect it should be possible to lift the jar by the lid. If the lid comes off, the seal is imperfect, and the fruit should be eaten within a few days or re-sterilised. Store in a cool, dark place. Remove the screw-band which may rust if left on the jar. Grease and store them for future use.

USING CAMPDEN TABLETS

This method is suitable for most stone and soft fruits, provided the fruit is sound and not over-ripe. Fruits not recommended to be preserved by this method are blackberries, cherries, pears, dessert apples, blackcurrants and gooseberries.

Dissolve the tablets in cold or tepid water, allowing 1 tablet to each ½ pint water. Pack the fruit in the jars, but do not pack too tightly. Pour in the solution until the fruit is entirely covered. At least ½ pint of solution must be used for each lb. of fruit and sometimes more is necessary. Seal at once with screw-band. If metal covers are used, the metal must be protected by 2 or 3 layers of paper fitted into the lid or by smearing the inside of the lid with vaseline. This method does not produce a vacuum, so it is not possible to test after sealing.

The fruit can be used for stewing, in puddings, pies, or for jam making. The fruit should be poured into an open pan and heated until there is no further smell of sulphur. If difficulty is experienced in getting rid of sulphur fumes in the case of plums, remove the stones first. Do not throw away the liquid as this contains some of the fruit juices, sugar and protective substances.

*Freezing fruit*

Most fruit freezes well, and this provides the best way of retaining a fresh flavour without altering the character and texture of the fruit. In a busy time, fruit may be frozen ready for jam-making at a later date. Ordinary jam-making recipes can be used, but it is advisable to use 10 per cent more fruit when frozen fruit is used (e.g. use just over 4 oz. extra fruit to every 3 lb. fruit in recipe). For later use, it is often sensible to prepare fruit in a variety of ways, e.g. unsweetened, in syrup or as purée to save time in preparing different recipes.

APPLES

Use firm apples for freezing in slices and fluffy apples for purée or sauce. For slices, peel and core fruit and put into a basin of cold water, then slice medium apples into twelfths, large ones into sixteenths. Use a dry sugar pack for preference (8 oz. sugar to 2 lb. fruit).

APRICOTS

Peel, halve and stone, and pack in dry sugar (4 oz. sugar to 1 lb. fruit) or in a medium sugar syrup. Fruit can also be packed in syrup in slices, or prepared as sweetened purée with the addition of a little lemon juice.

AVOCADOES

These are not really good for freezing because they discolour easily. Rub halves in lemon juice, wrap in foil and pack in bags. Dip slices in lemon juice and pack in rigid containers, or mash to a pulp with lemon juice (1 tablespoon to 1 avocado).

BANANAS

Not very useful in the freezer, but they can be frozen as a purée. Mash 3 breakfastcups of banana pulp with 8 oz. sugar and 3 tablespoons lemon juice and pack in small containers.

BLACKBERRIES

Use fully ripe, dark glossy berries, and discard pippy or woody ones. Wash well in chilled water, and pack dry and unsweetened, or in dry sugar pack (8 oz. sugar to 2 lb. fruit) or in medium syrup.

BLUEBERRIES

Wash in chilled water and drain thoroughly. Crush the

fruit slightly as skins toughen on freezing. Pack dry and unsweetened, or in dry sugar pack (8 oz. sugar to 2 lb. fruit) or in medium syrup.

CHERRIES

Red varieties freeze better than black. Firm the cherries in chilled water for 1 hour, dry and remove stones which may flavour the fruit. Pack in rigid plastic containers, as the acid in cherry juice tends to remain liquid in freezing and may leak through cardboard containers. Pack in dry sugar (8 oz. sugar to 2 lb. stoned cherries) or in syrup. Use a heavier syrup for cooking cherries.

CRANBERRIES

Wash firm glossy berries and drain. Pack dry and unsweetened, or as sweetened purée.

CURRANTS

Black-, red- and white currants should be stripped from stems, washed in chilled water and dried. Pack dry and unsweetened or in dry sugar (8 oz. sugar to 1 lb. currants).

FIGS

Wash fresh sweet ripe figs in chilled water, removing stems and being careful not to bruise the fruit. Pack peeled or unpeeled in dry unsweetened pack, or pack peeled figs in a light syrup.

GOOSEBERRIES

Wash in chilled water, dry and freeze without sweetening. For future jam-making, freeze slightly under-ripe fruit. Fruit may also be frozen in medium syrup or as a sweetened purée.

GRAPEFRUIT

Peel, remove all pith and cut into segments. Pack in dry sugar (8 oz. sugar to 1 lb. segments) or in a medium syrup.

GRAPES

Pack seedless varieties whole, but skin, seed and halve other kinds. Pack in light syrup.

LEMONS AND LIMES
Peel fruit, cut in slices and pack in light syrup.

MELONS
Cut into cubes or balls, toss in lemon juice and pack in light syrup.

ORANGES
Peel and divide into sections, or cut into crosswise slices. Pack in dry sugar (8 oz. sugar to 1½ lb. prepared fruit) or in light syrup, or in slightly sweetened fresh orange juice.

PEACHES AND NECTARINES
These fruits discolour, so they should be prepared quickly. Peel, cut in halves or slices and brush with lemon juice before packing in medium syrup.

PEARS
Pears should be ripe, but not over-ripe. They discolour quickly and do not keep their delicate flavour in the freezer. Peel and quarter the fruit, remove cores and dip the pear pieces in lemon juice. Poach in medium syrup for 1½ minutes, drain and cool. Pack in cold medium syrup.

PINEAPPLES
Use fully ripe, golden-yellow fruit. Peel and cut into chunks or slices and pack in dry sugar (4 oz. sugar to 1 lb. fruit) or in medium syrup.

PLUMS, DAMSONS AND GREENGAGES
Wash fruit in chilled water, dry well, cut in halves, remove stones, and pack in medium syrup. Damson skins are very tough, and they are best frozen as cooked sweetened purée. Good eating plums may be halved and frozen in dry sugar (4 oz. sugar to 1 lb. fruit).

RASPBERRIES AND LOGANBERRIES
Discard hard seedy fruit and wash in chilled water. Freeze dry and unsweetened, or in sugar (4 oz. sugar to 1 lb. fruit).

RHUBARB
Young pink sticks can be frozen unsweetened for pies, packed

in cartons or in polythene or foil. If lightly blanched for 1 minute, stems will pack more easily. Fruit may also be packed in medium syrup, or as cooked sweetened purée.

STRAWBERRIES

These are best frozen dry and unsweetened as they will be less pulpy when thawed. If packed in dry sugar or syrup, slice or lightly crush fruit (allow 4 oz. sugar to 1 lb. fruit). A delicious flavour and colour is retained if strawberries are sieved, sweetened to taste and frozen as purée.

### *Fruit Syrups*

Fruit syrups can usefully be made from a glut of soft fruit, to serve as a basis for winter drinks, and to use as sauces or to flavour mousses and ices. Bottles tend to burst or corks to pop out, and it is best to use the lever-stoppered type with a china cap and rubber washer; the second choice is the traditional sauce bottle with screw top. Syrups need to be sterilised, and should then be stored in a cool dark place so that the colour does not fade. It is far more convenient to store syrups in the freezer. These should be made to the same recipe, cooled and poured into containers, leaving room for expansion, then frozen. Small quantities of syrup can be frozen in ice-cube trays, and each cube wrapped in foil for storage. Each cube will be enough for 1 portion to dilute with water for drinks.

Syrups can be made from raspberries, strawberries, elderberries, blackberries, loganberries, blackcurrants, or a mixture of fruit. Use clean ripe fruit, and avoid washing if possible. Add a little water to the fruit (about ¼ pint to 3 lb. raspberries or strawberries, but ½ pint to the same amount of blackcurrants). Cook gently for an hour, crushing the fruit at intervals. Drain through a jellybag overnight, then measure and add ¾ lb. sugar to each pint of juice. Strain and pour into bottles, or into freezing containers. Make sure the bottles are securely topped and tied down. Stand bottles in a steriliser and fill with cold water to cover. Heat slowly so that the water reaches 175°F (simmering point) in an hour. Continue at this temperature for 30 minutes, remove bottles, cool and store.

*The Everlasting Rumpot*

One of the oldest ways of preserving fruit is in alcohol, such as a basic eau-de-vie, brandy or rum. This method can still be used in spite of increasing costs because the results are so delicious and so useful. The fruit should be sound, whole and ripe (but not over-ripe). If chemical sprays have been used, the fruit should be carefully washed and wiped, but fruit from the garden need only be wiped. Only choice fruit should be used, and the rumpot should not be overloaded. The only fruits to avoid using are citrus fruits, apples, bananas and pears.

When the fruit has been preserved, it has many uses and is a wonderful standby for making exotic puddings. The fruit may be eaten as it is, or with cream or yogurt; if the fruit is chilled it can also be added to a fresh fruit salad made of oranges, apples and nuts. A melon or pineapple may be cut in half and scooped out, then filled with some of the preserved fruit and its syrup—if small holes are pierced in the melon or pineapple flesh with a knitting needle, the juices will soak in to the flesh. The drained fruit can also be used to fill a flan case, or sponge, topped with whipped cream. For a really rich pudding, drain the fruit from the syrup and reduce the syrup in a heavy saucepan until it is thick. Mix it with sour cream and pour over the drained fruit, then chill well so that a rich caramelised mixture results.

To make the rumpot, a stone crock or large stone jam jar will be needed over which a cover can be tied. It is best to start the rumpot with the first fruits of summer such as strawberries, so that additional fruit can be added right through the summer and autumn.

INGREDIENTS
1 bottle light or dark rum
granulated sugar
fruit

Wipe the fruit gently, but do not peel or stone. The exception is melon which should be peeled, seeded and cut into large chunks. Put the fruit in the jar with its own weight of sugar and cover with rum. For each addition of fruit, add the equivalent weight in sugar, and cover with rum. Keep the jar tightly covered with paper and a lid, and store in a cool place. Keep adding fruit throughout the summer, and start eating it about Christmas—just take out as much fruit and syrup as required for each meal. Good fruits to use include strawberries, cherries, apricots, raspberries, plums, redcurrants, blackcurrants, peaches, grapes and melon.

*Candied Fruits*

Candied or glacé fruits can be prepared from many fresh and canned fruits. When dried out in an oven, they are sometimes known as crystallised fruits, or when rolled and coated in sugar. Suitable fresh fruits are cherries, grapes, oranges and pears, pineapple and stone fruits. Canned apricots, pineapple, pears, mandarin oranges and lychees are also very good, and process better than fresh fruit. The syrup should only be used for one type of fruit.

Good quality fresh fruit should be gently cooked in water until just tender before processing. Canned fruit should be drained from its syrup. Fresh fruit should be processed with a syrup made from ½ pint water and 6 oz. sugar to each 1 lb. fruit. When using canned fruit, allow 1 lb. fruit to ½ pint liquid made from the syrup and any necessary water.

Heat the syrup and use it to cover the fruit completely, keeping the fruit submerged with a saucer over the liquid if necessary. Leave to stand for 24 hours. Drain off the syrup, add 2 oz. sugar and dissolve. Boil and pour over the fruit. Repeat this process twice more, adding 2 oz. sugar each time. On the fifth day, add 3 oz. sugar, and boil fruit for 4 minutes. Leave for 2 days. Repeat the process and leave the fruit to soak for 4 days. Drain off the syrup and put the fruit on a wire rack (such as a cake rack) to drain and finish off in a very cool oven or a warm airing cupboard for about 3 days. Store in boxes with waxed paper in a cool, dark dry place.

Good candied fruit should be firm outside with a succulent interior, of a bright colour and sweet but true fruit flavour.

CANDIED APRICOTS

4 lb. just-ripe apricots
4 lb. sugar
1 pint water

Cut the skin carefully at the top of each apricot and squeeze out the stones. Make a syrup with sugar and water and when it starts to thicken, add the apricots and bring to the boil. Remove from heat, then bring to the boil again. Do this three more times, then pour fruit and syrup into a bowl and leave overnight. On the next day heat the syrup and fruit and boil for 1 minute. Drain the fruit and put into a bowl. Boil the syrup and pour over the fruit. Leave overnight. Repeat this process twice more until the apricots are saturated and the syrup has been absorbed. Place apricots on a rack covered with paper and dry in the sun or in an open oven, turning the fruit occasionally. When dry, store in a tin or wooden box.

CANDIED CHERRIES
2 lb. firm black cherries
2 lb. sugar
1 pint water

The cherries should be weighed after stoning. Dissolve the sugar in the water over a low heat without boiling. When the syrup is clear, put in the cherries. Simmer very gently until the cherries are almost transparent. Drain the fruit and put on flat trays. Dry thoroughly in the sun or in a very cool oven with the door slightly open. Dust with icing sugar containing a pinch of bicarbonate of soda and store in a box with waxed paper layers.

CANDIED ORANGES
6 medium oranges
sugar

Make a small neat hole at the top of each orange and scoop out the pith and pulp with a small spoon. This pulp can be used for another preserve, or for ice cream, which could be used to fill the candied orange shells for a special occasion. Soak the orange skins in brine made from ¼ oz. salt to 4 pints water for 7 days. Drain and soak the skins in fresh water for 3 days, changing the water each day. Make a syrup in the proportion of 1 lb. sugar to 1 pint water, and boil the orange skins until they are clear. Drain and put on paper on a cooker rack until they lose their stickiness. Serve at the end of a meal on their own, or filled with ice cream or an orange mousse.

CANDIED GRAPEFRUIT PEEL

thin-skinned grapefruit
sugar

Take the rinds from the grapefruit and cut into ½ in. strips. Cover with cold water, bring to the boil and simmer for 5 minutes. Strain and return to the pan. Repeat process three times. In the final process, simmer the rinds until tender, strain and cover with cold water. Drain and weigh the rinds and weigh an equal quantity of sugar. Using the drained grapefruit liquid, make a syrup with the sugar. Simmer until syrup is clear, then add peel and boil until the syrup is thick. Drain the grapefruit peel on a wire rack in a very cool oven with the door open. Roll peel in granulated sugar with a pinch of bicarbonate of soda. The peel can also be dipped in melted plain chocolate to serve as a sweetmeat.

CANDIED ORANGE AND LEMON PEEL

oranges
lemons
sugar

Remove the peel carefully from the fruit, if possible in quarters. Put the peel into a pan with enough water to cover and simmer for 1½ hours, adding more water if necessary. Add 2 oz. sugar for each fruit used and stir until dissolved. Bring to the boil, then put aside without a lid until the next day. On the next day, bring to the boil and simmer for 5 minutes. On the following day, simmer until the peel has absorbed nearly all the syrup. Drain the peel and put on paper on a cooker rack. Cover with greaseproof paper and dry slowly. A little syrup can be poured into the hollow of the peel pieces.

*Fruit Pastes*

Fruit pastes or leathers are made from fruit pulp cooked with an equal weight of sugar until the mixture is very dry and firm. It can be finished off in hot sun or in the oven and will store well between waxed paper in tins.

### APRICOT PASTE

ripe apricots
sugar

Take stones from the apricots and cook them with as little water as possible to prevent sticking. Put through a fine sieve and weigh the pulp. Mix with an equal quantity of sugar and heat and stir until all the moisture has evaporated and the mixture is dry. Roll the paste on a sheet of paper sprinkled with caster sugar, and leave to dry in the sun or in an open oven. The paste should be leathery so that it can be rolled up.

### QUINCE PASTE

quinces
sugar
icing sugar

Do not peel or core the quinces, but cut them into small pieces. Simmer in water just covering the fruit until very soft. Sieve the pulp and take an equal weight of pulp and sugar. Put them into a thick pan and stir over a low heat until the mixture dries and leaves the sides of the pan clear. Cool slightly and then roll out ½ in. thick on a board dusted with icing sugar. Stamp out rounds and leave them to dry, turning often until they are the texture of leather. Dust with icing sugar and store in tins.

Apple Paste and Pear Paste may be prepared in the same way. The mixture can be dried out on the rack of a cooker, or in a cool airing cupboard.

### REDCURRANT OR BLACKBERRY PASTE

2 lb. redcurrants or blackberries
sugar
½ pint water

Heat the currants or berries in water until they burst and are soft. Drain through a jelly bag and weigh the juice. Take an equal quantity of sugar and heat slowly, stirring all the time until the mixture is thick and dry. Put the paste into a baking tin and sprinkle with caster sugar. When cold and hard, cut into pieces with a knife, dip in caster sugar and store in a wooden box lined with greaseproof paper.

# Index